MANUALIA 30
UNISA 1985

THE SAGA OF GOD INCARNATE

ROBERT G CRAWFORD

UNIVERSITY OF SOUTH AFRICA
PRETORIA
1985

ISBN 0 86981 309 9

Printed by
Gutenberg Book Printers
Pretoria West

Published by the
University of South Africa
Muckleneuk, Pretoria

The publishers are indebted to the Editors of the Scottish Journal of Theology and The Expository Times for permission to print some material from essays previously written by the author for these publications.

To Pat and Paul
with much love

The old objection:

"Everyone saw his suffering, but only a disciple and a half crazed woman saw him risen. His followers then made a God of him, like Antinous ... . The Christian idea of the coming down of God is senseless. Why did God come down for justification of all things? Does not this make God changeable? Why does he send his Son into one corner of the world and not make him appear in many bodies at once?"

Celsus (circa AD 178)

"It is not (the mode of idea) to lavish all its fullness on one exemplar ... it rather loves to distribute its riches among a multiplicity of exemplars which reciprocally complete each other."

D.F. Strauss (1808–74)

The new objection:

"... It is more reasonable for us to see the doctrine (of incarnation) as an interpretation of Jesus appropriate to the age in which it arose than to treat it as an unalterable truth binding upon all subsequent generations."

Maurice Wiles (The Myth of God Incarnate, 1977)

Foreword

During 1982 the Department of Systematic Theology and Theological Ethics of the University of South Africa enjoyed the privilege of having Dr. R. Crawford as a guest lecturer for six weeks. His manuscript on the English Christological debate had reached an advanced stage and we were able to profit therefrom in lectures and seminars. Because the Theological Faculty at the University of South Africa is ecumenical it follows that no theological perspective can hope for general acceptance as a matter of course. It was a particular privilege to see how well Dr. Crawford coped in this particular open situation.

A number of aspects which struck me during the seminars will also emerge in the book. First of all he patiently, carefully and sympathetically discussed positions with which he disagreed. He always conducted himself calmly, revealing a healthy self-confidence. What further struck one was that in presenting his own point of view, Dr. Craword responded to other positions in depth. One got the impression that he exposes himself to the contemporary ferment and seriously seeks to profit from the current debate. Again, one was impressed by the way in which Dr. Crawford drew on the history of theology as he received the present debate and formulated his own point of view. I have no doubt that his position merits serious consideration and count it a privilege to be involved in the publication of his book in South Africa.

PROFESSOR ADRIO KÖNIG
Head: Department of Systematic Theology and Theological Ethics
UNIVERSITY OF SOUTH AFRICA.

Contents

Preface *(xi)*

CHAPTER 1
Who is this Jesus? **1**

CHAPTER 2
The saga of the Incarnation **8**

CHAPTER 3
How does God act? **18**

CHAPTER 4
Jesus: God and Man **36**

CHAPTER 5
Pluralism and Secularisation **55**

APPENDIX 1
Past controversies and the present problem **66**

APPENDIX 2
Christology **78**

Notes *90*

Index *103*

Preface

In 1977 and 1979 the publication of such books as *The Myth of God Incarnate* and *Incarnation and Myth* caused great theological debate and controversy in England and elsewhere. While some feared for the traditional doctrine of the Incarnation, others welcomed the opportunity of examining afresh the belief that is central to Christianity.

The purpose of this book is to continue the debate by examining some of the questions raised by the *mythographers,* as they have been called, and to make suggestions for the understanding of Christology in a more modern way. Further, to widen the scope of the debate by including the thought of some German theologians who might offer a solution to our understanding of Jesus.

In Chapter One the questions posed by the mythographers are raised and their objections to the traditional doctrine are discussed.

Chapter Two considers the use of the term *myth* in connection with the Christian doctrine of Incarnation and argues that this causes confusion and that a more appropriate term would be *saga.*

Chapter Three examines some of the problems that a modern historian might have when he studies the biblical material, and how he might consider an *act of God* to be possible today.

Chapter Four continues the historical approach and then moves the discussion into the area of philosophy. The theme here is how we identify people, and if philosophical insights can be useful when we try to construct a portrait of Jesus based on the Gospel narratives. It is contended that such a portrait gives us an *action Christology* which can be related to the traditional view of Christ.

Chapter Five examines some of the problems of Christianity in a world where knowledge of other religions has greatly increased and where many societies have been secularised. It is argued that the uniqueness of Christ can be safeguarded in such an environment.

The first appendix deals with controversies about the status of Christ in the centuries immediately preceding our own which bear a certain resemblance to the current debate.

The second appendix traces the historical background regarding the problems of Christology, considers some modern attempts at a solution, and thus to clarify more fully what has been stated in Chapter Four.

The writer wishes to acknowledge his gratitude to a number of people and institutions who, in various ways, have made the writing of this book possible.

In 1980–81 a Sabbatical year from the Open University and Brighton Polytechnic initiated the research, and a Fellowship from the University of Cape Town helped with the funding. Here thanks is due to Dr. J.C. Parkinson, Deputy Director of Brighton Polytechnic, who was very helpful in arranging the Sabbatical, and to the members of the Department of Religious Studies of the University of Cape Town for their friendly welcome and discussion of the research project.

Lectures on the theme were well received by Faculty and students at the Universities of Rhodes, Stellenbosch, Pretoria and Unisa and the University of the North. Gratitude is expressed for these invitations and for the fruitful discussions that ensued.

In the early part of the year a short visit was arranged by Professor Karl E. Nipkow to the University of Tübingen, Germany, and appreciation is due to the members of Faculty there who gave of their time to discuss the debate.

At various times Professors J.K.S. Reid, F.F. Bruce, William Neil, and A.M. Hunter, read the manuscript and thanks is recorded to them for their encouragement. The Rev. Dr. Paul Avis is also thanked for his help in suggesting how a first draft, a rather technical manuscript, might be recasted to reach a wider readership.

Appreciation too is expressed to Mrs Shaan Ellinghouse, secretary of the Religious Studies Department, University of Cape Town; and to Mrs Pam Turner and Mrs Betty Greeves of the Humanities Department, Brighton Polytechnic, who typed the manuscript at its various stages.

Finally, much gratitude is expressed to Professor Dr. Adrio König, Head of the Department of Systematic Theology and Theological Ethics of the University of South Africa, for his kind invitation to lecture on the theme in 1982 and his support in having the manuscript published.

BRIGHTON, 1985

CHAPTER 1

Who is this Jesus?

The authority and relation of Jesus Christ to God has always been a subject of debate. From the first centuries until now controversy has raged about his status. Orthodox belief placed him in the Trinity but Unitarianism thought of him as a man fulfilling a prophetic role. Those who were called 'Non-Subscribers', because they would not subscribe to creeds and confessions of faith in the centuries immediately preceding our own, occupied a middle position, holding to the Arian belief of the fourth century that he was a kind of demi-god. Anti-Trinitarianism appeared too among various groups during the Reformation, despite the protests of Luther and Calvin.[1]

Again, in this second half of the twentieth century, the dispute continues. Is Jesus, as traditionally defined in the creeds, God incarnate or is he, "a man supremely conscious of the divine presence and approved for a special role within the divine purpose."[2]

Some current English theology has put forward very persuasive arguments for accepting the latter position. Let us consider some of them.

Our century has witnessed the most amazing advances in science which, using the method of observation and experiment, has removed much ignorance and superstition. In particular, it has demonstrated that what previous centuries considered supernatural and mysterious can be explained by natural causes. We need not now think of God breaking into the natural order to perform nature miracles or cure diseases for we know both causes and remedies. Of Man it can truly be said that "he has come of age".[3]

Further, our world has grown small in that speed of travel has brought the most remote near to us so that we know more about the culture and religion of other people than at any other period. Such contact, both at home and abroad, has widened our spiritual and mental horizons so that we need no longer believe that Jesus is the way for all people to follow in their search for God.

Moreover, historical and critical study of the Bible has shown that we must not understand it too literally. This was the mistake of those who constructed the creeds and confessions of faith and erected metaphysical doctrines on the basis of statements which should have been understood mythically. Particularly, in their reading of the Gospels, especially the Fourth Gospel, they mistook the metaphorical and mythical for the literal. Again, they read into the titles given to Jesus a status and authority which was not there originally; a truer reading indicates that he is more likely to have been "a charismatic prophet".[4]

The creeds, however, insist that Jesus was both God and man. But this belief has never been capable of rational demonstration even on the basis of the concept of 'substance' which was part of the world view of the later Roman Empire, for it involves contradictions which cannot be resolved. Would it not be better to think of a unity of activity of the divine and human in the person of Jesus: a homopraxis rather than a homoousia?

Further, the credal position has often led to an exaggerated stress on the divine nature of Jesus and a diminishing of the humanity which has resulted in a cult of the divine Christ. We need to recover the humanity of Jesus and see his divinity in terms of his "God-consciousness".

In order to arrive at such a conclusion we must try and understand the nature of religious language. Here a key term will be "myth" and what it signifies. Myths, it should be observed, can be either true or false. They are often used in connection with the origin of things. Hence the stories in the opening chapters of the book of Genesis are regarded as myths, but they have a true significance for the theist, namely that the world is dependent upon God. But it is not only in connection with creation that "myth" proves its value for we can apply it to the whole of divine action in understanding the significance of Fall, Incarnation, Atonement, Resurrection of the Dead and Final Judgment.[5] Each of these, given the proper interpretation, can have a "true" significance, but often a false "myth" has been attached to them.

Here, it is argued that the traditional interpretation of the person of Christ falls into the latter category for it saw a metaphysical identification of Jesus with the second person of the Trinity. This raised not only Christo-

2

logical problems, as we have seen, but introduced mythical (in the false sense) notions of a pre-existent divine person who came down from heaven.

In addition to myth the use of metaphor in religious language must be understood. When someone embodies some ideal or idea or attitude or value in his life we can think metaphorically of it being incarnated in that life. For example, we say: "Iago was malice incarnate" or "Joan of Arc incarnated or personified the resurgent spirit of France" or "Winston Churchill in 1940 incarnated the defiance of the British people." Thus when we say that Jesus was God incarnate we mean, not that he was literally so, but that the divine love or attitude to mankind was personified or incarnated in the life of Jesus.[6]

Of course the divine agape or love is incarnated in every act of self-giving love to some degree but in Jesus it was, 'incomparably greater' so that the incarnation is a matter of degree and no longer confined to one example.

When we say: "Jesus is the Son of God" we should remember that we are dealing with a metaphorical and not a literal statement. The origin and development of the term 'son of God' confirms this for in Hebrew thought the king is regarded as the son of Jahweh by adoption (Ps. 2.7). There is no physical or metaphysical connection with God. Thus in thinking of Jesus, especially if we set aside the later Virgin Birth stories, we might see the adoption of Jesus as son in the account of his baptism where one of the ancient adoption formulae used at the coronation of the king is spoken.

Myths employ metaphors and what they are trying to do is to produce a particular attitude in those who understand them. To hear the king spoken of as a son of God would produce a particular attitude in his people (one could also think of the divine right of kings in English history) and similarly when Jesus was thought of in this way it produced a particular attitude in his hearers.

In general they saw him as the agent of God carrying out His purposes. He was supremely open to God and to man so that he showed both a profound human response to God and a loving outreach of God to the world.[7]

This is further confirmed when we pay attention to parable and symbol in the Bible. Parables and symbols represent or stand for something; they are not the 'thing itself'. The Life of Jesus is a parable where we seek for meaning not fact; it is a symbol pointing to God.

These poetical images in which the Bible abounds mean, when properly interpreted, that the world is a carrier of spiritual value and Jesus has absolute significance as a human ideal. He is the true pattern of human

3

living and must surely inculcate in us the desire to follow in his steps. In fact we could go as far as to say that the love of God expressed itself through him supremely and that the power of God was at work in a new way through his life and ministry.

This is not to say that God has expressed himself through Jesus exclusively, as some aspects of the traditional view contended, but that it was one point at which God has acted. Such a position will make inter-faith dialogue more possible and enriching.

But is not the life of Christ unique because of his resurrection from the dead? No, because in those pre-scientific days the idea of resurrection was commonplace and therefore it must be doubted whether the resurrection event, whatever its nature, was seen by the contemporaries of Jesus as guaranteeing his divinity.

What we must grasp is the determining role that the environment played in the development of Christianity. We must not project our ideas into the minds of the first disciples and apostles. They were 'primitive' men who lived in a world where the concept of divinity was commonplace and where another deity would not be out of place. Similarly, the Fathers and Apologists of the early centuries of the Christian faith produced doctrinal beliefs which reflected the outmoded Greek philosophy of the day. How can such concepts have meaning for our age?

Up to the seventeenth century the idea of God breaking into our time and history was acceptable and the Christian apologist could see in miracles the credentials of the faith but against the background of modern science, developments in the study of history, especially in the nineteenth century, saw history as a continuous and unbroken nexus of cause and effect.

This reflects the evolutionary view of the world which has come to see continuity and development as keys to the understanding of life on earth. There can be mutations and novelties but they are explainable in terms of heredity and environment. Events differ in degree but not in kind. Hence current theology tends not to accept one event which is said to be of a different order of decisiveness and uniqueness than other events.[8]

Myth is connected with the general and universal not with the particular. Hence, if we use it as our frame of reference, the act of God is seen in more general historical experience rather than a particular event which traditionally has been called Incarnation.[9]

Of course the historian who comes to the study of Christianity has difficult problems: his struggle to remain objective, the nature of the sources (preaching rather than historical writing), and the uniqueness of the events described. On this latter point, to say that the historian deals with unique events and that therefore Christianity does not pose a problem, does not really solve the difficulty. In dealing with other occurrences no matter now unique they are the historian has something with which to compare. They are unique in degree but not in kind, whereas Christianity in traditional form contends for a unique Incarnation which is different in kind from other events.[10]

Modern theology can also point to the problem of the resurrection in this context for here we have another unique happening. Jesus himself passes through death to a new kind of life. The historian, assuming a general consistency in the way the world behaves, looks for a natural cause (hallucinations or visions on the part of the witnesses of the event) rather than a supernatural miracle.

Or if these explanations do not seem completely satisfactory he decides for agnosticism. He confesses "I cannot explain it." Modern theology, having every sympathy for the dilemma of the historian, points to the fact that it was the disciples who had the experience of the 'Easter appearances'. Their vision was structured by their faith for it is faith that enables men to see visions. A religious vision gains its content from the previous life and thought of the person who experiences it, hence the New Testament Christophanies hark back, in a great deal of detail, to the earthly life of Jesus. Only someone who knew that life could have had such an experience.

Hence, we must conclude with Bultmann that the resurrection means "the rise of faith" in the risen Lord. This is much easier to communicate to the modern mind than some extraordinary miracle which contradicts the laws of modern science.[11] Jesus, during the forty days was at work in the minds of the disciples by his spirit, producing faith in them. Otherwise, the resurrection understood as an objective fact of the restoration of the man Jesus is a nature miracle which cannot be demonstrated to the modern mind. What we must do is to demythologize it with the interpretation which we have noted above. The resurrection is not an objective event about Jesus, but a statement about the inner life of man.

The problem, however, arises out of the difficulties caused by restricting the action of God to particular events and a particular person instead of resting belief on a more general historical experience. This would not exclude giving Jesus Christ a very high status in the sequence of historical events.

We can think of him completing and resolving Israel's religious history by discovering the true way to God and giving it definitive expression in his teaching. Filled with God's spirit, he was the first discoverer and pioneer of salvation and the anticipator of the end of all things.[12] This gives him a supreme, if relative, place.

With regard to the act of God we can say that it takes place in worldly occurrences in a hidden manner which does not affect the closed web of cause and effect. We experience the purposive activity of God in such events and can regard them as in some way "special".[13] If asked to define "special" we might say "in the sense of being more fully expressed." Thus the life of Jesus more fully expressed the purpose of God than any we have known. In fact we might speak of him as final in the sense that all God's promises and purposes find their fulfilment in him.[14]

How is it then that some people see in Jesus such an expression of God's purposes and others do not? The reason may lie in terms of response which reflects their personality and situation.

Again, our definition of God will determine how we think He acts in history. If He is completely different from us we can imagine Him acting in an extraordinary way and even breaking the laws of the Universe which He himself has instituted. But if we proceed from man by analogy to God then on the basis of our knowledge of the human self (relational, social, changeable) we can think of God as having the same characteristics but at a much higher level. This God is finite, primus inter pares, but definitely related to our time and history. We might say that He tries to realise Himself in the world. Hence there is no problem about his action in the temporal sequence and since He is continually relating himself to the world there is no problem of an incarnation viewed as an exclusive act.[15]

Again, our view of God's action will be determined by our view of man. If we think of every man as to some extent God's act since all creatures have their basis in God's free decisions and creative actions then the action of God in Jesus Christ while in some sense special, is immanent in the creative process.

Hence, the emphasis of theology in the second half of the twentieth century has been on the immanence of God rather than his transcendence. This shows the influence of the evolutionary world view and the endeavour to see God as active in the process. God has been in immanent relation with the cosmos from the beginning so that we need not think of his action as arbitrary and extrinsic. Here Jesus Christ is taken as a significant clue or key to the cosmic drive.[16]

Such proposals by modern theology should elicit our sympathy, for the emphasis which traditional theology has placed upon the uniqueness of the events of Christianity poses, as we have seen, very difficult problems for the historian. He proceeds by criticism, analogy and correlation. Thus the principle of analogy rules out a priori such an event as resurrection, for the historian has nothing with which to compare it. Modern theology solves this problem by understanding the resurrection not as a literal or historical event but as an event which has an existential meaning; that is, 'awakening faith' in the life of the individual in the present.

Further, if we think of all of history having a meaning or reflecting the divine, we shall not be setting ourselves the difficult task of demonstrating the certainty of particular events such as those centring around the life and death of Jesus.

One must appreciate this attempt of modern theology to redefine the authority and status of Jesus Christ for it is not always appreciated how perplexing and difficult the traditional 'substance' Christology is and how illogical it appears to the modern mind.

Hence current theology advocates an 'action' Christology rather than a 'substance' one. If this can communicate with the modern world in a better way without losing the essential content of the Christian message it would be great gain. Further, an attempt to state such Christology from 'below' i.e. beginning from the humanity of Jesus, would remove many of the problems which are created by a Christology from 'above' i.e. starting with the divinity.

In summary, modern theology is raising questions and offering answers to problems which in various forms have been asked from the beginning: How does God act in history or in the world of nature? What is the nature of the evidence for such an act? How is the Bible to be interpreted in a modern scientific age? What is the nature of religious language? Can we speak of a unique act of God in a relative stream of history? What is the relation of such a unique act to other acts of God as witnessed to by other religions?

Two main problems confront us before we can consider the place of Jesus Christ today. First, religious language, and secondly, the relation of Christianity to history. In our next chapter we shall consider then, such terminology as myth, metaphor, symbol etc and ask how they are to be used in interpreting the biblical evidence and how relevant they may be in understanding the act of God in Jesus Christ.

CHAPTER 2

The saga of the Incarnation

Modern English theology contends that the belief that Jesus of Nazareth, while being fully man is also fully God, arose because the Bible was interpreted too literally. It is argued that passages in the Bible which imply such a doctrine should be seen as mythical or metaphorical expressions which properly interpreted mean that Jesus was a human ideal: the true pattern of human living reflecting both the love and power of God.[1]

Myth dramatises in narrative form a moral or spiritual truth and has the purpose of enforcing faith.[2] Thus the "truth" of creation is not concerned with the beginning of the world in the scientific sense but with the spiritual insight that man lives in dependence upon God.

However that may be, we need at this point to consider some of the difficulties in the use of myth. While we can accept immediately that myth is often used to enforce a spiritual or moral truth there are problems when it is applied not simply to particular biblical stories but to the person of Jesus Christ. Myth has a timeless character and this is an immediate defect if we are going to apply it to a story that has a historical basis.

Further, in this connection, it is not an appropriate word for mass communication. If it is the business of theologians and clergy to communicate with as wide a public as possible then the use of a term which in every day speech means 'non-existence' is inappropriate.

Again, the difficulty is not lessened in academic circles where different definitions of the word circulate. With regard to theology, problems have arisen from the use of the term by Rudolf Bultmann as we shall see.[3]

Literature of course abounds in myths. They inspire men to fulfil their dreams and aspirations for they portray heroes who stimulate the imagination of the reader and make him want to emulate their exploits.

Moreover, myths are often explanations of origins i.e. creation. They may arise, however, from man's actual experience of himself as he contemplates his dependence and weakness in the face of evil. The myth seeks to explain how these conditions have arisen and represents real elements in the human psyche.

Myth is universal. The events occur in 'The Great Time' and are independent of the changes wrought by historical processes. It makes use of symbols which stand for various features of the world and symbolic objects which possess a supernatural potency.[4] Myth, too, with its strong stress on the imagination has been used to express truth beyond the power of reason as in 'The Myth of Er' at the end of the Republic of Plato, i.e. the vision of life after death.

It has a connection with legend, but the latter term has a basis in history, for it is an elaborated story about real events and carries a local interest for a particular tribe or people. Thus myth could be used in connection with Adam as a universal concept (אָדָם =humanity) and legend with regard to the Hebrew patriarchs, i.e. Abraham, Isaac, Jacob etc.

However, since legend in common parlance often finds itself in the same category as myth, fable and fairy story, it is better not to use it in connection with the historical.

What term then can we employ in connection with the gospel narrative? We would suggest the term 'saga' for a number of reasons. It is a term which suggests a reality of some kind to the modern mind. It is used by the media and in everyday conversation.[5]

Saga is the old story of Scandinavia which describes the people of northern Europe. It is the story of a particular people containing legend, myth, symbol, metaphor etc. But it is connected with history and the particular, whereas myth is often a symbolic story about mankind in general whose goal is to represent eternal reality and universal truth. Thus the danger of applying myth to the incarnation is to suggest that the incarnate life of Christ and his redemptive work are types or helpful representations of what is universally true of human experience.[6]

9

Saga is realistic narrative. It is a way of depicting a situation or character in a 'life-like' way i.e. richly, colourfully. Such a narrative is confined neither to an historical nor ideological dimension, though it is involved in both. It is a mode of writing which takes up a position somewhere between life and literature. It views the real world, but from a certain distance neither too far away nor too close by. Being neither philosophy nor history it maintains 'a middle distance': this 'delicate meeting place between imagination and knowledge.'[7]

If this view of the gospel narratives was acceptable then it would have to be admitted that historical criticism of them had taken a wrong turn. Its whole emphasis was on the historicity of the gospels. In part this perspective was praiseworthy, for it recognised that the material was 'history-like' but made the mistake of treating it as strictly historical without recognising that it could have a meaning independent of this criterion. The whole intention was to sift out the historical from the non-historical:

> "The realistic or history-like quality of biblical narratives, acknow-
> ledged by all, instead of being examined from the bearing it had
> in its own right on meaning and interpretation was immediately
> transposed into the quite different issue of whether or not the realistic
> narrative was historical."[8]

This approach does not oppose historical criticism but argues that it may be too dedicated to detail and accuracy that it cannot discern the 'wood' because it is too occupied with the 'trees'. It seeks to discern patterns in the gospel narrative which reflect intention/action sequences in the life of Jesus. It preserves a 'middle distance' in viewing an agent or character, recognising that this is necessary if he is to be rendered vividly. Its perspective is neither too far away nor too close by. Assuming that the full scope of the Gospel story is needed to give us the continuity of the identity of Jesus it shows that Jesus showed a dedication to the will of God that was unsurpassable. His intentions and actions were closely identified with the intentions and actions of God and that was particularly demonstrated in the passion narrative. Both the stories told and the structure of the narrative indicate that he knew how to behave as God's son even if consciously he was unaware that he was God's son.[9]

The picture we have of Jesus is derived from a collection of stories or to put it more strongly, the picture is the stories. It is fragmentary, lacking in continuity and inner coherence from a biographical standpoint, yet there is a unity: the story of saga seen as a single whole. It is the structure which gives the unity and the patterns that structure the story so as to give an identity description of a single agent.

Moreover, it can be shown that stories about Jesus enacting human intentions are consistently related in certain patterns to stories about how he enacted divine intentions. It is the biblical patterns themselves that set a limit to the imagination of the theologian.

Perhaps at this point we might refer to a modern biographer seeking to render a realistic picture of his character. He interviews him on many occasions and seeks to gain a general understanding of what he is like. As he listens to the stories that he tells of his experiences he is not so sure of the factual detail of the account. Here he is faced with a dilemma. Is he to cut out those myths that have developed in the telling or is he to see them not as simply adding colour to the narrative but as bringing out the meaning in a deeper way? Those who have written biographies of modern characters have often defended the latter course either because they were not sure what was fact and what was fiction or, having gained a general understanding of the character, they realised that both were needed to depict the person as he really was.

Form Criticism has told us that we cannot know what Jesus was really like since the historical picture is seen through the eyes of the early Church. But what if the Church having gained a general picture of what Jesus was like, told stories about him that were helpful for their own particular needs (*Sitz im Leben*) which, though not strictly historical, reflected how they knew he would have behaved in a particular incident?

The stories had to pass the criterion of the basic picture of Jesus which had been handed down to them and had to conform to what they knew of his character and conduct. The fact that the stories in the so-called apocryphal gospels failed to pass that test and were not admitted to the canon of scripture is well known.

Realistic narrative then, is not identical either with historical or mythological literature. The gospels have kerygma (preaching) and affinities with religious and mythological literature of the Near East, but they are distinctive narratives in their own right. They portray ordinary and creditable individuals rather than stylised or mythical hero figures. This is a strong characteristic of realistic narrative. Extraordinary themes with analogies from workaday occurrences are expressed in ordinary talk, i.e. the parables of Jesus.

Today it is recognised that one way to identify people is to tell stories about them. What we do, when asked to describe someone in more detail than a simple description of physical characteristics, is to relate stories that illustrate his behaviour.

The Gospels are a portrait of Jesus in which his words, acts and sufferings are described in saga-like realistic stories. Perhaps the best parallel is the historical novel which often conveys the portrait of a person or period better than a conventional history. Four versions of the Gospels imply creative reconstruction but they serve to identify Jesus and display basic agreement. The fixity of the canon indicates that the rendering of Jesus given in these stories is the best available. Creative imagination need not be discounted for it is something that the historian needs to do his work.[10]

In short then, we must not fall into the trap of hastily making history the test of such realistic stories. As Brian Wicker writes: "Perhaps it is only now, as a result of our long experience of reading novels, that in narratives which once again combine the empirical and the fictional in a mode of narration more complex than either of these can be by itself, are we able to recover the true nature of narratives written before the split occurred." And as Ford notes: "Any simple separation of fact from fiction is especially difficult when it is a matter of conveying a vivid character. How important is the verification of details when they are being used as part of a complex synthesis to portray an individual? Given that the rendering does not contradict known facts, but embraces them, of what might falsification consist short of giving an alternative portrayal which would raise the same problem?"[11]

One additional point may be made here about saga. While it is a record of the past which makes contact with history and uses a historical background as its framework, it does not hesitate to adjust and order historical detail and events to its own use, namely, the significance and meaning of these events. Thus we have the theological interpretation of the Fourth Gospel.

Further, while saga is history in the sense of being 'history-like', its purport lies in the present and the future.[12] It gives an account not only of the past but of how things are now and provides paradigms for future hope. As James Barr points out, the story of Abraham was told not because the writer wanted to communicate how things had been in the second millennium B.C. but because he wanted to provide a paradigm for a promise that was yet to come. Thus if the Hebrew/Christian tradition claims in some way to be historical, it also claims to be eschatological.[13]

Hence that aspect of modern theology which has stressed the need for an existential interpretation of the Gospel story as relating to our present existence, though it has often been criticised for its neglect of history, has at least pointed to an important emphasis of the narrative. Further, those theologians who have reminded us of the eschatological nature of the message of Jesus have, as we will see, something very important to say about his person and work.

12

If we then apply saga to the story of Jesus on the basis that it has a frame-work of history, what of other matters such as creation and consummation? Should we use saga here too? An argument can be brought against this. The term refers to a human hero and his deeds and therefore cannot be used of creation and consummation, for these are pure acts of God. It is argued therefore that saga should not be used at all but myth for all three acts of the divine drama.[14]

This argument is understandable, for it insists that the use of different terminology might separate events which are related to one another and therefore threaten the biblical picture of God's dealings with man.

However, we tend to reject it for the following reasons. In understanding the way of God to man in Christianity, we must start with the act of God in Jesus Christ. Otherwise we tend to fit it into our view of creation. Further, such an act is different from the other events since it happened in human history and took place in connection with events of which we have some documentary record. Saga too, as we have argued, involves memory and a purport for present and future and all of these were involved in the Church's image of Christ.

Further, a historian can investigate such realistic narrative, as he will do with historical novels concerned with the period which he is investigating, but with events such as creation and consummation he is dealing with something quite different. Those who have used saga in connection with creation have admitted that the historian does not investigate such an event, for their definition of saga differs from ours in that they speak of a 'pre-historical reality'.[15]

In sum then, since creation and consummation are 'before' and 'after' history as we know it and are not tied to a particular historical event, we would not rule out the application of myth to them as long as it was accepted that they contained some 'ontological' element.

Evolution could be regarded as the process of creation, and creation itself as the 'willing' and 'purposing' of God. Without such will and purpose such an event would not have taken place. Thus the theist distinguishes himself from the atheist or materialist who speaks of the universe as self-evolved without indications of will and purpose. Such a materialistic idea is based on a mechanical view of nature and at times is expressed in the statement that the universe is an 'accidental collocation of atoms'.

The Fall of man has its 'ontological element' either in the sense that something went wrong with a good creation or that 'every man is the Adam of his own soul'.[16]

In any case the state of man both in the first century and, as we can note, in our own case today, required an act of redemption and reconciliation which made necessary the life and death of Christ. Saga is a better term to describe such an event for it relates to an historical life and death and holds together metaphor, symbol, fact, myth.

However, whatever terminology is used, the crucial matter is interpretation. Current theology does not intend to eliminate myth (David Strauss 1808–74) but interpret it. This interpretation is based on the views of certain biblical scholars but this leads to an impasse, for other scholars see the evidence in a different way. The basic problem revolves round the question: What kind of reality are we dealing with: God become man or a man supremely conscious of the divine presence?

Let us illustrate this by referring to metaphor. In the previous chapter we noted that current theology says that the statement: "Jesus Christ is the Son of God" is a metaphor analogous with the statement, "The king of Israel is the Son of God", which indicates that both were adopted by God.

Here we note first of all that a strict distinction is being made between a literal and a metaphorical statement. Some writers relying upon what is called the tension theory of metaphor would agree and would go on to say that a literal or factual statement has truth claims that a metaphorical one does not possess. It is contended that metaphoric language has a contradiction which makes it difficult to decide its truth or falsehood. We should regard it as emotive or subjective. Thus what the metaphor does is to produce an attitude on the part of the person who makes the statement.[17]

But many metaphors have a literal meaning or interpretation. For example: "the chairman plowed through the discussion" can be replaced with the literal statement "the chairman dealt summarily with objections or ruthlessly suppressed irrelevancies". Or, "sleep knits up the ravelled sleeve of care", can be replaced by "as a result of getting a good night's sleep a careworn person will be less disturbed and distracted by his cares."[18]

Modern theology too, despite its stress on the metaphorical rather than the literal, proceeds to give a literal equivalent of: "Jesus Christ is the Son of God", i.e. Jesus is the incarnation of the love of God. But, in so doing, it has departed from the analogy with the king of Israel! We were told that both statements meant adoption, but it could hardly be said that kings of Israel were the incarnation of the love of God! Hence, if we are

14

to accept that Jesus was love incarnate, something more needs to be said than adoptionism. Perhaps this helps us to understand why the Early Church rejected such a view of the person of Christ since it was inadequate to explain what they saw in his life and behaviour?

However: Was what they saw sufficient to turn the myth into a metaphysic?[19] Modern theology answers in the negative. It contends that where men and women have lived in self-giving love (agape), it has been incarnated in human lives so that the notion of incarnation (in this sense) is not confined to Jesus. But, and the further step is significant, it is also held that the divine was more fully incarnated in the life of Jesus than any other life, therefore Jesus is unique (degree not kind).

Of course modern theology rejects the metaphysic because it was based on Greek philosophy which is not acceptable to the current empiricist thought. It made possible various accounts of the person of Christ which today are unacceptable. We shall return to this problem in chapter four of this book.

But the illustration of the use of metaphor shows that there is a literal equivalent. Scholars who recognise that the statement "Jesus is the Son of God" is metaphorical, contend, after an exhaustive survey of the origin and development of the title 'Son of God' in Judaism and Hellenism, that its literal equivalent is "the origin of Jesus in God's being (i.e. his love for all creatures and his unique connection with God) and true humanity."[20]

Thus calling a statement metaphorical does not solve the problem of different interpretations. The tendency of current theology is to see Jesus embodying the love of God in his life and work just as we might say Churchill embodied the defiance of the British people during the war or Joan of Arc personified the resurgent spirit of France.

But there are certain difficulties here. While Joan expressed the resurgent spirit of France and Churchill the defiance of the British, it is obvious that there are other aspects of France and Britain that they did not reflect.

God, we are told, is love but also light, spirit, truth etc. Are we then to accept that while Jesus personifies the love of God he does not reflect these other attributes as well? Apart from being contrary to scripture, this raises the problem of how full the revelation is in Christ. Could it be that in many ways God is different (we are thinking here of the moral attributes of God) from his action in Jesus Christ?

Further, some thinkers in this current theology, question even the fulness of the revelation of God's love in Christ by doubting that such love was perfectly or absolutely embodied in every moment of the life of Jesus.[21]

However that may be, it does raise a problem for those who want to make unique claims for the humanity of Christ. Traditionally the perfection of the humanity could be deduced from his hypostatic conjunction with his divinity, but since modern theology rejects this they must find support for the perfection of his humanity on historical grounds. This, it is asserted, is not so easily done.[22]

The point is a significant one, for those who have denied the metaphysical uniqueness have too often assumed that they can demonstrate the moral uniqueness by considering the historical material available. That is why we have stressed that the gospels are saga, meaning realistic narrative, which seek to identify a person in all the various turns and twists of the crucial period of his life. It is on this basis that we shall seek to erect a Christology. The emphasis will be on the portrayal of this person by the narrative as a whole and not on the truth or falsity of any particular stories or texts.

However, it must be admitted that this general picture does not escape the 'truth' problem. But in answer we could make a number of points. Firstly, it is necessary to overcome the modern tendency to see truth as a 'paring away' and to accept that it may be a 'gathering together': "a process of accretion which may appear to lead to paradox and contradiction, but which, in the end, resolves them by asserting completeness..."[23]

Secondly, a story may be true in the sense of 'true to life or experience.' In such a story, as the gospel narratives give us, the characters are credible and offer a glimpse of human nature as it is.[24] The saga has a dimension which reflects the truth about human nature for the past, present and future.

Thirdly, saga by weaving together history, teachings, theological ideas, myths etc may uncover 'the essence' of something or somebody in a way that a strict historical account could not do. The latter would give us 'truth' in a secondary way; it would be a copy of the original and imperfect, "since a personal life can never be fully captured in words."[25]

Thus John Macquarrie considers the gospels analogous to works of art and in some cases art-works of genius. By way of illustration, he refers to the account of the trial in the Fourth Gospel. "If there had been a clerk of court who had left us a transcript of the trial, it would have probably read very differently. But John, by what Bultmann calls 'a remarkable inter-weaving of tradition and specifically Johannine narration', has dramatically

16

presented the essential meaning, which is a reversal of the roles of Jesus and his judges, so that it is the political and ecclesiastical establishments that are shown to be on trial."[26] And, we might add, subsequent generations have fully accepted the 'truth' of John's claim.

Having said that, however, and having in this chapter touched upon the relation of saga to historical truth, we need to go more deeply into the problems facing the historian as he seeks to examine the gospel narrative. In so doing we may be able to underline once again the advantages of regarding it as realistic narrative.

In the next chapter we shall raise the following questions. How far is the job of the historian simply the uncovering of bare factual details about Jesus and not the investigation of the Church's interpretation? How far does his scientific world view prevent him from engaging in such an examination because the claims of the Church are so improbable? Is it true that "the greatest story ever told" is unlike most other stories because it conflicts with the normal assumptions that the scientist makes about the world we live in?

Many people want to believe in such a saga since it brings hope for the present and the future, but how can they accept an act of God as described by the gospel narratives? This, as we will see in our next chapter, is the problem facing the historian.

CHAPTER 3

How does God act?

We noted in Chapter One that some current theology sees the action of God as taking place in the general course of history rather than being restricted to special events or particular individuals. It is contended that no one individual takes an absolute place in this general stream of history so that we might say of him that in some way he is God incarnate.

Further, it is maintained, that such a view of revelation will contribute a greater degree of certainty to faith than seeking to rest it on what has been called 'the scandal of particularity'.

In this present chapter we want to examine these views but we need to set them in the wider context of some of the problems that face the historian as he considers the biblical material and we require to understand the scientific, philosophical, and theological factors which are involved.

1. The historical approach

We can define 'history' in two ways: what actually happened in the past or the attempt by the historian to reconstruct the past. Basically, it is accepted nowadays that the latter meaning pertains to what the historian actually does.[1]

The distinction is worth making for sometimes writers on the Gospels tend to give the impression that because we cannot actually know what happened in Palestine in the first century we should abandon the attempt. But, if the material does reflect the authors' attempt to reconstruct the past then

18

it must be regarded at least as 'history-like'.

This means that the Gospels and other New Testament material are not free from the subjective element, i.e. they are not unbiased or uninfluenced by personal feeling or belief.

Again, this element has been regarded with suspicion by some scholars who want to get at what they call the 'facts' and discover that they cannot penetrate through to what actually happened because of the Church's interpretation.

But since history is the historian's interpretation of the past he can never totally eliminate the subjective factor. The historian can never really free himself from the 'hidden influence' of his own environment and prejudice. He can only seek to minimize it.

A more pertinent objection to a historical investigation of the biblical material is that such ancient attempts to reconstruct the past bear little resemblance to the technique of the modern historian who is guided by definite rules of establishing fact, interpreting evidence, dealing with source material, etc.

However, it is doubtful if most historians would make such a rigid distinction between writers of their craft in the past and present, for if they did they would have to deny the title 'historian' to some of the really great figures of the past.[2]

One of the real differences is the modern historian's sympathetic rapport with the past, seeking to bring about a dialogue between past and present, and not attempting to judge the past from a point of superiority to it.

He sees clearly that each age has something to teach us. Hence he will be interested in the first century and may approach it with the sympathetic understanding that it was an age of intense religious feeling and enthusiasm which may have something to impart to his more secular environment. He will be particularly interested in the charismatic figure of Jesus and the community which came into being. He will study its Founder in the context of his social environment and will ask if the current ideas of the time could have caused the Christological development. In some ways, as we noted in Chapter One, current theology accepts this as the cause of the development, but the historian may ponder over this assumption and may decide otherwise, i.e. that the early Christians used the terminology and beliefs of their age in order to communicate with their hearers but reshaped them for their own purposes.[3]

Further, history contains narrative which tells a story and has a movement through time and it has explanation and analysis. The Gospels, (apart from analysis in the modern sense), do display these features but there is difficulty in establishing when events took place. Chronological and geographical factors are often subordinated to theological purposes. Hence it is not unreasonable to conclude that they are not a history in the modern sense but have a historical connection. At the same time they do not pretend to be a biography.

Again, especially if they are taken in a literal way, they have a pre-scientific view of the cosmos. This appears to influence current theology in many ways and at times leads to the conclusion that we cannot accept what they say about the supernatural.[4]

With the shade of Augustus Comte (1798–1857) hanging over him the historian might be tempted to arrive at a hasty judgment here. Comte saw history developing in three stages: superstitious or theological, metaphysical, and scientific. In this view the biblical record would fall into the first period as relevant to its time but not to ours. However, to accept this would be unhistorical, for it puts forward abstract and general laws of history instead of trying to understand what actually happened.

The historian differs from the social scientist (Comte is often regarded as the Father of sociology) in that he is interested in the particular and unique rather than the common factors and regular patterns which are discernible in man's activities in society. He is very aware that particular circumstances never occur in exactly the same way and he is therefore concerned to highlight differences. Parallels and generalizations can follow but he must start with particular examples.

This must mean an interest in the person of Jesus for it is generally admitted that he was in some way unique. Hence the historian cannot approach the study of such a person on the basis of recurrent patterns in human activities and try to fit Jesus into them.

On the basis then of a strict historical examination he may arrive at the following understanding of Jesus: He was a teacher and a prophet and was credited with miraculous cures. Nowadays it is generally accepted that these cures attributed to Jesus were far less common than used to be thought and were for the most part without precedent in his own culture. They do evince a "style of activity that demands serious explanation."[5] He was, too, a controversial figure, especially concerning the Law, and he was a preacher of the kingdom of God. Much controversy centres about this concept as used by Jesus, but it is generally accepted that he saw it in an apocalyptic context. We shall have cause to return to this element later.

Moreover, there is evidence that he required some decision from his hearers concerning himself and his work. Finally, his death was a well attested fact and was probably due to the belief of the Jews that his activity and teaching was a threat to them.

Much more, of course, could be said concerning the activity of Jesus, his disciples and the people that he associated with, but we want to concentrate on other elements which puzzle the impartial historian and which he may eventually dismiss as either impossible or incredible.

We do this because such 'supernatural' elements in the Gospel story, regarded as 'violations of natural law', are often dismissed out of hand or as reflecting a superstitious age. If, on the other hand, there was even the slightest degree of probability in, for example, the resurrection of Jesus, it would have a tremendous impact on how we regarded him. That is to say, if there was some objective element in the event and not simply subjectively interpreted as 'the rise of faith' in the early disciples.[6]

With regard to the 'healing miracles' which we have just mentioned, there is not the same difficulty. The historian knows of psychosomatic medicine and he is aware that sickness is often related to the mind. Further, he remembers that the *Society for Psychical Research* has, despite considerable opposition over the years, reached its centenary year. It has had a host of illustrious members and a wealth of meticulously documented material, and public opinion polls taken in recent times have shown that paranormal phenomena are now accepted as 'normal' by eight out of ten people in Britian. Telepathy, the action of the mind on matter, psychic forces, etc. are more generally recognised now than they were in the days of William James and Henry Sidgwick.[7]

Hence the cures attributed to Jesus could have been possible, but what of such a unique event as resurrection? The historian proceeds by the principle of analogy, i.e. comparing the known with the unknown, but with what will he compare the resurrection? It is absolutely unique, for 'dead men do not rise.'[8]

Nevertheless, there is biblical material that reflects a witness to such an event and the historian cannot allow his enquiry to ground to a halt without investigating it.

The earliest writing about the resurrection occurs in the fifteenth chapter of Paul's letter to the Corinthians. The sources used are very early. It is very likely that an old Aramaic formula forms the kernel of the tradition containing verses 3b—5. Paul then expanded this with the 'appearances' reported in verses 6f, presumably with information which he had received on his visit to Jerusalem. The ancient formula itself could have reached back to the first five years after the death of Jesus.

It is clear too that Paul himself was very close to this event. According to Gal. i.18 he was in Jerusalem three years after the conversion and visited probably James and Peter from whom he must have heard concerning the resurrection. If his conversion is to be dated, from the information in Gal. i, in the year 33, and the death of Jesus is to be put in the year 30, then Paul would have been in Jerusalem between six to eight years after the events.

Thus while Paul himself was not a witness to the resurrection, apart from his vision of the risen Jesus on the Damascus road which changed his life, he nevertheless wrote after conversing with those who had been. His close proximity then to the event would recommend him to the historian.

Again, our previous mention of 'paranormal' experiences would have a bearing on the thinking of the historian since it deals with the objective reality of unusual occurrences.[9]

On the other hand, he cannot rule out 'hallucinations', 'visions', etc. which could account for the belief. It might be argued that the past experience of the disciples had led them to expect that this would happen. In short: we see what we expect to see. This, however, goes completely against the picture presented by the biblical record which shows a group of scattered, despairing and disillusioned disciples.

However, human nature being what it is, it might be contended that the disciples had something to gain in putting forward such a belief. It is natural to contend for what we believe even when others regard the cause as having failed. But this doesn't seem to explain matters either. They were Jews and all their past experience mitigated against a human individual such as Jesus entering into the 'new life' of the Messianic age before it was brought in by divine intervention. In fact, the Christian movement offered no distinctive advantage or novelty, but had the disadvantages of exclusion from Judaism and scorn or death from the pagan world. Movements which hold false notions survive but they usually have certain advantages to offer to their adherents.[10] If they had a 'dead body on their hands' (some still maintain that the disciples stole the body) what was the point of their dying to contend for the contrary?

But perhaps they were deluded in some way. After all, current theology argues that it was a superstitious age where resurrections were common-place. We need to be careful about this 'pre-scientific' concept, however, for the ancient Greeks had developed quite a sophisticated scientific view of the world.[11] But let us accept that this was generally correct.

The historian then, as he puzzles over the preaching of the early Church, would expect that the message of the resurrection would be acceptable. But the Sadducees could not accept the idea of resurrection and proceeded to have the disciples arrested. (Acts 4.3) At Athens, when Paul argued for the resurrection he was greeted with mockery (Acts 17.32) and when he told the Jews at Jerusalem of his change of life, which had happened through his vision of the risen Jesus, they cried: "Away with such a fellow from the earth! For he ought not to live." (Acts 22.22) In short, riot and uproar greeted such a message in a world where we might have expected such news to be commonplace!

At this point the historian could conclude that some abnormal or unusual event had occurred which produced a community willing to die for the belief. As to the nature of the event he considers that he must remain agnostic for he cannot explain it.

However, he realises that it is the understanding of scientific law which precludes acceptance of such an event and that therefore any attempt to say more about it must pay attention to what science is saying today.

2.   The transformation of the scientific world view

It is generally accepted that the seventeenth and eighteenth centuries thought of the world as a machine which, after it was designed, did not require any outside interference with it. This immediately raised problems for the action of God in nature and history, for it placed Him as First Cause beyond the world and a spectator of its activity, i.e. Deism.

Newton, while accepting the mechanical order of the cosmos, did recognise that a different kind of cause was needed for the creative process that is 'an agency of will'. He thought that 'irregularities' and 'unexplainable factors' required God to maintain balance and harmony. This had the unfortunate consequence of imagining God as the One who supplied answers to things which science could not explain i.e. 'God of the gaps'.

Further, scientific concepts such as mass, space and time were regarded as literal representations of the world and the observer was independent of them.

But Newton's basic point was significant for theology: the impossibility of reducing the universe completely to a mechanical system. Hence, it is in some way contingent, that is having no self-subsistence and no ultimate stability of its own.

However, his concepts of space and time which he regarded as absolute prevented him from accepting the traditional doctrine of the Incarnation. He held that God contained the universe (the container notion of time and space) just as a pail contains water. Since a pail cannot become part of the water which it contains, God cannot become part of the world, i.e. Incarnation.[12]

Today, however, the scientific picture has changed. Nature is no longer looked upon as mechanical particles determined by fixed laws but as governed by statistical laws which do not determine occurrences of single events but only proportions in the larger classes of events.

We must look at what this means in more detail. Physicists have been forced to re-examine the basic concepts and ideas by which they have understood natural events. For example, it was noted that the observer is involved and not merely a passive spectator and that his observation altered the position of the object. When he examines a billiard ball, for instance, the ball did not move but its primary nuclear particle 'jumped'! In fact it became difficult to know how nuclear particles would behave under certain conditions and observations.[13]

The behaviour of minute particles in the atomic sphere cannot be predicted for they seem to behave in an irregular and arbitrary way. Laws can only be determined when these particles are observed in great numbers in the systems as a whole instead of singly. Hence the concept of statistical law which indicates probability, not certainty.

This new insight into the nature of matter has led to the "abandonment of the deterministic world-view" in physics and "has made it more difficult to regard the existing state of science as finally legislative of what is and what is not possible in nature."[14]

Further, since the knowledge of psychology and sociology is still very limited and if, what has been traditionally called 'miracles' are regarded as 'social phenomena of great complexity', it is difficult to know what 'laws of nature' would look like in this area and even more perplexing to know what a 'violation' would be.[15]

Laws of nature of course are based upon observation, experiment and experience. On the basis of the latter we expect that when A appears B will follow, but this is not always so. Better weather can normally be expected in England in June rather than December, but then the unusual happens in a certain year: a mild December and a bitterly cold June. The uniformity has been broken. The meteorologist can give us reasons as to how this has happened but why it has occurred is more difficult. On the basis of past observation he can argue that it is unlikely to happen again but, since he cannot observe the future, he cannot say for certain. On the basis of observation and experience all we can say is that A is normally followed by B, but there may be exceptions to this regularity.

However that may be, science is also based upon experiments which take place under certain controlled conditions and they are repeatable. In order to prove or disprove something experiments are performed again and again. It only requires one exception to arise to disprove a law, provided that the experiment can be repeated.

But miracles are not repeatable. They are particular and peculiar events occurring, as we have said, in human situations: ".... they are not small scale laws. Consequently, they do not destroy large scale laws."[16] Moreover, the biblical record indicates, that they are not random or arbitrary events 'without rhyme or reason' but occur in a sequence of events and relate to the self-disclosure of God. We shall return to this point at a later stage.

An event then, such as the resurrection, is unique and unrepeatable. But it is not sufficient reason to abandon natural law, for to do that it would have to be an experimentally repeatable exception: ".... the miracle does not fall into this category, otherwise it would itself be a new small scale law, not a 'violation' of regularity."[17]

In sum, this argument, if acceptable, means that miracle has the peculiar power of violating but not destroying a law of nature. Whether or not, of course, a miracle occurs depends on the evidence. A wise man, as David Hume (1711–1776) would say, proportions his belief to the evidence. This is somewhat different, however, from saying that miracles do not happen because of an a priori ruling that they just cannot happen. The evidence for each occurrence must be carefully sifted and reasons given for the supernatural or mythical or naturalistic explanation.

Now, while we cannot base these 'exceptions', which do not destroy laws of nature, on the new picture of the world, we can at least say that, if Heisenberg saw indeterminacy as a real feature in nature which falls outside the state of affairs to which causal and necessary laws apply,[18] then the novel, unusual, unexpected event may not appear so improbable as in the Newtonian machine – like universe.

The new model of the cosmos is more like an organism than a machine. In the evolving universe there is the emergence of new levels of organism: matter, life, mind; and organisms themselves have higher and lower levels. Even an animal is regarded as more than a collection of physical and chemical reactions. A certain creative activity is discernible, for the animal can change both environment and feeding habits. Further, in seeking to understand the animal it is necessary not only to examine the parts but the creature as a whole. Physiologists can examine the parts i.e. the circulatory system but cannot explain the whole in terms of this. Again, the survival of an animal does not rest only upon its physical make-up but also on its behaviour: in some senses the higher animals appear to be able to 'choose', i.e. element of will involved. "But if consciousness plays a real part in the process and if the end products are conscious creatures capable of understanding their own development, in what sense can the whole process be called blind?"[19]

The end product is man. Here, it must be admitted that viewed on the lower level a certain mechanical operation takes place due to his hereditary and environment, but also on the higher level a transcendence which can be regarded as the self with the exercise of free will.

Now if, as we have argued, there is a certain indeterminacy in atoms and we can see a certain freedom in animals then we would expect man to display this to a much greater extent.

This is not to contend for dualism, that is a separation between mind and body so that the first is not determined and the second determined, as Descartes (1596—1650) contended.[20] Such a 'ghost in the machine' is not acceptable in view of what we have said about the psychosomatic, that is the interaction of mind upon matter and how closely they are related.

We might consider this thinking and willing as the 'within of things': the psychic side, which apart from inherited instinctive behaviour, may be independent of the DNA code that governs the form of the physical frame though it interacts with the physical system.[21]

This 'independence' gives me the feeling that at times I can stand 'outside' my physical make up, without 'violating' the laws which govern it. Certainly I am held responsible for initiating events, and though I may plead heredity and environment as mitigating circumstances, I am still held responsible in the legal and moral sense. We must now see how we can relate this to theology.

3.   The theological viewpoint

Let us move from man and his relation to his body to God and His being related to the universe. I pervade my body and I am at one with it yet I think of it as obeying my will and purpose. Using this analogy I can think of the being of God including and penetrating the whole universe, so that

26

every part of it exists in him but that his being is more than, and is not exhausted by, the universe.[22]

This has the advantage of preserving both the transcendence of God (beyond the world) and His immanence (within the world). The latter can be stated as God's organic relationship to the world and the former as his monarchical relation.[23] The danger of certain types of theology is that the emphasis on immanence in the process has led to postulating a finite God whereas the danger of the monarchical model is a God completely external to world, i.e. Deism. Only if we hold a strict balance between the two do we do justice to the biblical record. God is the high and holy One who dwells in eternity, according to the prophet Isaiah, but He is also the One who dwells in the heart of the humble. (Is. 66 : 1—2)

God acts in the past, that means the doctrine of an initial creation, but also in the present bringing in the new i.e. creative activity. But He is also involved in the future.

There is always a flaw in human analogies but let us attempt one. We speak of the creative activity of the writer and musician. The writer uses 'words' but what are they? Certainly not "spatio-temporal pre-existing material". A creation out of 'nothing'?[24] A writer and a composer have these creative ideas before they write or compose. What is the time sequence of such a creation? It can happen over a long or short period of time.

How can such creative 'acts' be understood? We can examine *when* the story was written, *how* in the sense of the words used and the development of the plot, *what* cultural factors contributed to the process, but the actual creative activity is a 'leap beyond the facts' as we can empirically observe them. Such creative activity is not unscientific, for many biologists collected facts before Darwin but his theory, while based upon the facts, went beyond them.

Further, we need to distinguish between creating and making. The creative ideas may be 'still born' and never be written or the music never composed. Again, some creators leave the work of execution to others, there is even the hint of this in the biblical record of the creation of the world: the concept of Logos or Word of God. But here the Logos is so closely identified with God that the distinction is blurred. (John 1. 1—2)

Again, the creator remains 'outside' the work when it is finished but he is 'within it' in the sense that something of his personality or even his very being has gone into it. The work reveals its creator, i.e. the music of Chopin is easily distinguished from that of Beethoven. Hence, the Psalmist, too, is convinced that the cosmos reveals the glory and handiwork of God. (Ps. 8 : 1—3)

27

Further, discords and defects can become obvious as the music is executed. This may have many causes: the poor performances of the players due to misinterpretation or even a lack of understanding on the part of the creator. The Hebrew/Christian traditional answer to the problem of evil has been the former rather than the latter. It is held that the creation was good until the main performer tried to make himself like the creator and fell into sin and misery.

But it is inconceivable that any writer or composer once the defects have appeared should not seek to reorder, rearrange, recreate. Great composers and writers strive for perfection. Can we think of God doing less? Thus the Christian tradition of incarnation, redemption, consummation.

The analogy of course fails in many points, perhaps most of all, due to model of the world as an organism, for here we can think of God pervading in a much more pervasive way than the composer or writer.[25]

Organisms, as we have said, have higher and lower levels where the novel and unusual takes place in patterns of behaviour that are related to the lower levels.[26] On the higher levels at times the unusual takes place: a real change. When this is difficult to understand it could be said that the activity of God takes place as an additional factor. This activity is not easily discernible, but neither it is easy to understand how the creative ideas of the composer or writer are formed.

In man in particular, as the one made in the image of God, we would expect this activity of God to take place. What if then an individual in the higher levels of his being was to achieve a unique unity of will with God? Such a unity would be so extraordinary that we could expect him to accomplish what the biblical record reports concerning Jesus.

In the world there is evidence of order but also disorder. As it has often been said: "Nature is red in tooth and claw". Suffering abounds everywhere and while there are other aspects of good and order in nature it is now admitted that the Cross pattern which Christianity has emphasised is "deeply woven into the very fabric of creation".[27]

Everywhere we see disease, violence, death. We protest about this, wrestle with the philosophers to explain the problem of evil, sympathise with and encourage the medical research that tries to alleviate disease, but death remains: the greatest mystery of all. Why should it be so unfair and unjust, cutting off lives when they have only begun to flower? We know instinctively all of this is a 'violation' of the good creation.

Hence we would expect the good Creator to reorder, rearrange, recreate. What if we viewed the acts of God in Christ in this light? If he reached the unique position of an identification with the will of God then, "where God is perfectly obeyed", the mechanics of the material world may "look different from what they do in a situation dislocated by disobedience".[28] This as we have argued would not destroy the laws of nature for the events are unique and unrepeatable. It may be, however, that our idea of how things work is based on too narrow a set of data.

This, of course, makes two assumptions: firstly that God exists and secondly, that he has acted in a unique way in Christ. The latter assumption will be discussed in the next chapter, but with regard to the first, the existence of God is not in dispute in the current theology that we have in mind throughout this book, only his mode of operation, i.e. in what way he has acted in Christ.

But assuming that there was a unique identification of will between Jesus and God, what we shall seek to demonstrate in the next chapter, then what he did, "need only be what 'normally' happens – indeed what is bound to happen – on the rare and 'abnormal' occasions when a right relationship is achieved in the family of God."[29]

However, that may be, the acts of God happen in a context and relate to the past, present and future. Let us see this first in the history of Israel and then in the life of Jesus.

Israel saw the events of their history as having the form of promise and covenant. The exodus from Egypt was seen as the work of Yahweh who was not only the Lord of History but the Creator who was 'in the beginning'. Since He transcended history this gave Him a freedom to enter creatively into history. This God 'went before them', He 'lured' them on into the future.[30] Indeed it is not too much to say that He was "the One out of whose gracious creativity every new moment of the future was actively brought into being."[31]

This is what is called the eschatological element in the faith of Israel which was spoken of by prophet, seer and people as they looked forward to an end-time, a new age when God would be all in all.

The same element was present in the teaching of Jesus. Though scholars have difficulty about many of the sayings of Jesus and the titles that may have been ascribed to him during his earthy life, there is a strong body of opinion that agrees that Jesus did make a claim to authority and a demand for decision in relation to his person and message. He did this in an apocalyptic context: He claimed to usher in the 'end-time'.[32]

29

How are we to view this latter concept? Was Jesus mistaken when he spoke of the imminence of the Kingdom of God? This was the view put forward by Johannes Weiss and Albert Schweitzer at the turn of the century. They saw Jesus as an apocalyptic enthusiast whose thinking was animated by an expectation which has since proved to be an error.

But more recent German theology has taken a different view. The Jewish expectation was the resurrection of the dead at the 'end-time'. What if the resurrection of Christ was the anticipation of that end-time? In this case, while Jesus' expectation of the imminent end was not fulfilled in the world as a whole, it was fulfilled in his own person. This would mean that in Jesus the consummation has already taken place and his divine authority endorsed by God.

Here the difference between the Hebrew and Greek view of 'truth' is important. The Greek had a static view of the world and a cyclical view of history; the Hebrew had a more dynamic view of the world and a linear perspective on history. For the Greek the 'truth' was under or behind things, for the Hebrew 'truth' was found in history and revealed itself in the future.

The resurrection of Jesus is a foretaste (proleptic) of the end of history. Thus if the apocalyptic view of history is true it is not difficult to make sense of the resurrection of Jesus. But is it true? Some current theology finds this difficult to accept.[33]

Perhaps the first thing we might say about the apocalyptic perspective on history is that it relates to the nature of man.

On the basis of what we have said about the scientific world view it can be contended that the world is loosely ordered — an open universe. We could also say that organisms and their systems while related to lower levels are 'open' upwards.[34] This is reflected by man in particular who appears to have an openness beyond the world.[35] He also has an openness to the world. When he shuts himself up in anxious self-centreness he loses his openness to the world and this can lead to his self destruction.

If we interpret the 'image of God' as this openness to the world and to God, we might see the effect of the "Fall" in man as closing himself both to the world and God.[36]

But to preserve this openness man needs trust, hope, and love. These are characteristics of man and are directed to the future rather than to the past or even the present. It is 'hope' in particular that keeps man 'alive'; without it he becomes disillusioned, cynical and despairing.

Man feels too that life is too short for him to fulfil his work. Thus the desperate expedients made by some to prevent the ageing process and the mad scramble of others to get done what they feel must be accomplished.

Death makes nonsense of all promise and fulfilment. "Since man is open not only to but also beyond the world his hope for rational meaning in history leads him to a hope for fulfilment beyond history."[37]

This does not mean that we need to accept literally the symbols and thought forms of the apocalyptic but that we are obliged to take it seriously and to assess its rationality as an expression of the universal context of hope and faith within which all history can be interpreted.[38] In short, its essential meaning, though clothed in forms that we find difficult, is not foreign to us for it corresponds to the universally human. The same despair and hope prevails today and provides conditions in which similar aspirations are expressed by religious and secular writers alike.[39]

If man does not accept the Christian framework as the ground of his hope he will opt for a belief in progress or Kant's *Reich der Zwecke* (rule of moral ends) or communism. Man's hope accepts either a secular or religious structure for without hope he cannot live.

Moreover, the biblical eschatology is not so far away from modern thought as some theologians seem to think. Modern science sees the end of the world in a far more bizarre and dramatic way than anything that the Hebrew imagination could conceive. The Revelation of John is, "a pale document compared with these modern scientific apocalypses".[40] The biblical apocalypses (Mk. 13 and Revelation) address themselves to the same questions "as we now raise in the light of the scientific prediction of the end."[41] The difference is the gloom of the scientific picture as compared with the radiant hope of the biblical one.

But still, it must be admitted, that faith is resting on a certain view of history, on probability rather than certainty and it is giving prominence to a particular event. Let us consider the latter point first.

Certain arguments can be advanced for the particular:

a)   In the context of the revelation given to Israel it can be contended that some definiteness and completeness should be given to the divine overall purpose. Hence the event of a person which gave specificity and definite content to the concept of God and brought the revelatory process to its goal.[42]

b)   It is acceptable that an event can occur in a community which will change its whole way of looking at its history, it illuminates all other events and makes them meaningful. Thus religion, according to Alfred North Whitehead, appeals to direct intuition of special occasions, and to the elucidatory power of its concepts for all occasions. It arises from that which is special, but extends to what is general. Singularity and universality are fused.[43]

This event can rightly be called saga: it is a paradigmatic happening that has its roots in history but it is not an exact reconstruction of what actually happened but an expression sometimes in poetic form of a concrete person or event. Saga is not myth, it is a creative and interpretative response to an historical event which is a central focus of illumination for a community that provides the basis for interpreting life as a whole.

In fact, it is doubtful whether religions could ever become universal without the concrete individual and founder who becomes the focus of creed, cult and conduct.

To accept myth is to contend for the general rather than the particular but this is at the expense of the biblical witness, where the act of God is particularised and is different from that operative in the general run of worldly occurrences.[44]

c)   But the particular has specific reference and meaning for the general. Here the difference between the historian and the theologian needs stressing. The historian is interested in a limited and definite period and is inclined to see the idea of universal history in a somewhat speculative light, but the theologian is interested in specific events in relation to their meaning for history as a whole.[45]

The action of God takes place in such world history and is in continuity with it. Moreover, it is open to rational enquiry and requires the exercise of our judgement, but it also has an unpredictable nature, radical novelty and a relation to promises and expectation in previous history.[46] The novelty is particularly related to history rather than nature and is reflected in the new things which Israel experienced and compelled them to say: "This is the Lord's doing and it is marvellous in our eyes" (Ps. 118 : 23). But while new it is related to the past and the future. The promises made to the patriarchs became surprisingly new in the Exodus as to their fulfilment: the history of Israel is thus revealed as open to the future with the idea of God developing from involvement in their local history to the Yahweh who controls the destiny of the nations. The experience which they had of the world empires from the period of the Exile onwards made the sovereignty of God explicit and was expressed strongly in their apocalyptic writing, e.g. the meaning of history will only be fully known when the end of history has come. To present Jesus without this context is to go back to the nineteenth century lives of Jesus which endeavoured to present him in terms which modern Europe could understand. "His person was interpreted in terms of his moral character and the kingdom which he proclaimed in terms of progressive moral education".[47]

Again, this stress on universal history does not take away from the particularity of God's action for, "it is only in the context of the expectation (arising from the tradition) of God's future action in history that events have the character of divine self-disclosure. It was in Israel that this happened, but it happened in a way which refers to the whole of history. It is from the perspective of the tradition and history of Israel that this distinctive concept of universal history arose".[48] In sum, in Israel "all the families of the earth will be blessed (Gen. 12 : 3).

If, then, these arguments for retaining the particular in proper relationship with the universal are acceptable, what about the difficulty of resting faith on probabilities rather than certainties? Does this not make faith particularly vulnerable?

Here caution must be exercised concerning the meaning of certainty. There are degrees of certainty and the word is relative to the realm of discourse in which it occurs. For example, a mathematical statement has a different kind of certainty from a statement of empirical science. There is no such thing as absolute certainty this side of omniscience. Even in formal logic one can be mistaken.

In the Newtonian world view it was agreed that mathematical physics was, "the bedrock of the explanation of reality"[49], but now even mathematical models are problematical and uncertain. Euclid geometry does not reveal the properties of physical space. Einstein used curved Reimannian geometry though this is inconsistent with Euclidean geometry with respect to parallel lines but both have applications to the physical world. "Thus to the assertion that the structure of mathematics represents the logical form of the world we are entitled to ask, which mathematics?"[50]

Faith too is to be distinguished from the knowledge on which it is based. The logical and psychological relations of faith and knowledge are very important in this regard. Though a man may have only "probable" grounds for the resurrection of Christ, he may yet believe in the doctrine. How is this possible? At first sight it appears to be odd, and yet it is something which men can base their actions upon. Galloway points to the analogy of marriage: "A man, after reading the Kinsey report, may be objectively aware that there is a statistical probability that his wife is being unfaithful to him. This knowledge is both psychologically and logically compatible with a trusting belief that she is in fact faithful."[51]

This, as Galloway points out, does not make faith independent of knowledge, for trust where there were no rational grounds for belief would be sheer irresponsibility, but faith is compatible with the degree of uncertainty inherent not only in historical knowledge, but in all finite, human knowledge.

There may be a certain illogicality too about any demand for absolute certainty. If at this present moment we assert that the events recorded in the New Testament did not occur we need to know for certain that they did not. But it is asserted that we can never know anything for certain. How then can we know that such events did not occur? All that we can do is to put forward grounds for and against such occurrences.[52]

In conclusion we note that this discussion has shown that while history is related to Christianity it cannot demonstrate even in the light of the new scientific view of the universe, that it is true. It cannot give grounds for certainty and it has doubts about any belief (including communism) that sees history interpreted by a particular factor or person. Further its study is concerned with the past not the future. It can only testify to degrees of probability. But 'truth' is more the establishing of exact facts.

We must now draw this discussion to a close. It was necessary to examine some aspects of the historian's work in order to see how he might approach a record of events which are unusual and novel.

However, we saw that the biblical narrative referred not only to the past but the present and future. Hence the historian was limited in his task since he has not got the tools to enquire concerning present implications or the revealing of the 'truth' by the future.

Thus, the Gospels look more like realistic narrative, as we have maintained in a previous chapter, rather than simply concerned with past events. They have connections with history and this aspect needs examining with all the historical criticism and scholarship which is available, but they have in their own right a relevance for 'meaning' which we must not neglect in the interest of historical accuracy. They are more like literature, with its vivid portrayal of characters, the strength of their plot, and their compelling sense of reality.

Perhaps the inadequacies of the historical approach were most apparent in our discussion of the creative activity, which enters into the production of literature and music, for its tools are inadequate to discern thought processes and intentions. Here the insights of philosophy and psychology are more helpful.

As we will see, in the next chapter, this realistic narrative reflects intention/action sequences in the life of Jesus. These portray a person in terms of behaviour and provide material which can be brought into dialogue with current philosophical discussion concerning how we identify people.

The problem in short is to try and understand what kind of person Jesus was. If, it can be demonstrated that he had a unity of will with God that has never been surpassed, then what seems very unusual for us may have been possible for him. We cannot discover that by the historical approach alone, though we need to take it into account, in order to see if it can give us any grounds for 'probability' even in the weak sense of the term.

Historians will differ over 'probability' but if our arguments concerning its relation to 'certainty' carry any weight then we need to recognise that someone who has made such a unique impact justifies more than attention to strict historical detail for the rendering of the vividness of his character. Indeed, it might not be too much to maintain, that such a rendering based on 'probability rather than certainty' may give us a 'truer' idea of what he really was like.

CHAPTER 4

Jesus: God and Man

As the last chapter has made clear, one of the problems concerning the identification of Jesus is the nature of the evidence which is available to us. The Gospels are written from the standpoint of faith and are intended to create faith in those who read them. This has posed a problem for the historian, as we have seen, and can lead to the belief that we can never know Jesus as he really was.

However, the historian does not make the claim that what he discovers by exact historical enquiry corresponds with what actually happened at the time. Hence we can say that a 'historical image' of Jesus (if it is possible) is still as much an image as the believer's 'faith image'. "This at once relativizes the sharp contrast supposed to exist between the 'Jesus of history' and the 'Jesus of faith'. By way of 'image', they both derive from the 'earthly Jesus' ".[1]

Further, while we can apply the historical and scientific approach to the study of a person, this does not mean that these disciplines will uncover the person as he actually is. There is always the mystery of the person or the 'elusive self'.[2] How much more must this be the case in dealing with extraordinary characters in history?

Currently, however, the historical study of the Gospels has seen the lessening of the distinction between the historical 'Jesus of Nazareth' and the 'Christ of the Church'. This distinction has been stressed by Form Criticism (*Formgeschichte*) which looked for the seedbed of the Jesus tradition solely in the Christian community after Jesus' death and this entailed putting the main emphasis on the discontinuity between Jesus as a historical figure and the Christ proclaimed by the Church.[3]

While it is not denied that the Gospels reflect the views of the writers it is none the less thought that they, "contain sufficient information about Jesus and recollections of him, in respect of his message, his attitude to life and his conduct as a whole."[4]

Thus the historical approach can accept that the Jesus of Mark's Gospel is a figure of early first-century Palestine and not an invention of the late first-century Rome because of the language he uses, the traditional parabolic method of teaching, the claims made by him, and the hostilities he arouses. Again, the units of tradition on which Mark is based presuppose broadly the same Christ as the finished Gospel and other units, preserved independently in other places and used by other Evangelists, also presuppose a fundamentally similar figure. Hence the basic picture of Christ is carried back to a point only a quarter of a century or so after his death. Further, because of the retentive memory of the Oriental we can often be virtually sure that what the tradition is offering us are the authentic deeds, and especially the authentic words, of the historic Jesus.[5]

Of course, while the attempt is made to disentangle the historic Jesus and the Church's reaction to him, this does not mean, as D.E. Nineham points out, that they were wrong in their estimation of him i.e. if they assigned to him titles to which he himself laid no claim, these titles may still point to the truth about him.[6] What we have in short in the Gospels is an interpretation. However, if too much emphasis is placed on the accuracy of the narrative we may relegate the meaning to a minor place, and miss the point that ancient writers were more concerned with meaning (inculcating good example and moral virtue) than with truth in a modern historical sense. The view of each writer of the Gospels is reflected in the way he makes his characters behave, thus the different picture of both Jesus and his disciples in the four writings.

What is valuable in the historical approach that we now employ is that the differences are compared and the attempt made to get back to the original material of the tradition.[7] But this must be related to the ancient view that, "what matters is the truth of the story itself, that is, whether it 'turns us on', strikes home and makes us the active subject of a new story... it has to do with taking action, with a challenge or appeal or summons to a particular attitude...".[8] Hence both true stories in our modern historical sense and fictitious ones have the same function.

The argument that we have sought to sustain so far has been that the evidence before us is realistic narrative, i.e. recognising that the stories are 'history-like' and have a distinct meaning. What often happens, however, is that either the historical or the literary approach is emphasised to the detriment of the other. It is hoped that we might be able to maintain a balance between the two, paying attention to not only 'what is written' (meaning) but also 'what is written about' (truth).[9]

As Schillebeeckx points out, three questions then need to be asked of the evidence: What do the stories mean? What do they say to us? Did they happen? For some people if the last question is answered in the negative the first two have no relevance. But this is not acceptable. The 'truth' of the story of the Good Samaritan does not depend on the historicity of the event but its relevance to all men everywhere of the value of helpfulness. This was surely the intention of Jesus in telling it.

Further, if the Church inserted stories in the Gospels that do not belong to the original tradition and make comments on those stories, it does not follow that these did not represent the general picture of what Jesus was like. If some stories or events do detract from such a basic posture then Form Criticism can detect them and draw our attention to the inconsistency.

On the other hand, when the stories that are judged unauthentic conform to the general picture of Jesus then they are 'true in substance'.[10] "People have often been confused about the Formgeschichte terminology..." but "there is no intention whatever of denying that what is historically 'un-authentic' may nevertheless capture the deepest real intention of Jesus — only that in a purely historical sense this cannot be demonstrated."[11]

Thus, while not neglecting the question: Did they happen?, we can perhaps do more justice to the other two questions.

Before doing so, however, we need to consider how we identify persons. In general, identification takes place in terms of names, addresses, occupations. Further, identification indicates relationship in the family and social group at large. Thus we speak of someone as being the son of .... or the brother of .... or the father of .... or a Northerner or Southerner .... or working class or middle class ..... Today it is argued that a person becomes what he is in terms of his relationships. A positive or negative response to such relationships can determine both character and personality.

The danger of course is that the individual could be so merged with the group that he loses his identity but this need not necessarily follow. The individual can join groups and dedicate himself to causes without losing his identity. He can choose to withdraw from them when they begin to express values and attitudes of which he cannot approve.

Again, we identify people by their actions. We take account of bodily movements and can predict at times the effect of actions before they have been completed. While we cannot resolve a person into his actions we can discover what he is like from such activity. Of course, appearances can be deceptive and we must always be on the guard in case we misinterpret behaviour. Suppose I see a man in a darkened room lifting a glass to his lips. What is he doing: perhaps refreshing himself or toasting some achievement or even committing suicide? Only the intention reveals the action. Hence in order to understand him I need to infer his intention as well as observe his action. Traditionally philosophers have been inclined on the basis of Descartes' division of body and mind to separate intention and action, but today we argue that they go together, i.e. intention/action. Some philosophers have even gone so far as to say that a person's being is constituted and not just illustrated by the intentions which he carries into action.[12]

However that may be in describing a person we recount characteristic patterns of intention/action. As Barth says: "The being of a person is being in act",[13] but does this not mean resolving a person into his actions? Much current philosophical discussion centres around this question but Barth's via media appears acceptable. He does not contend for 'a real self' behind our actions or attempt to resolve the self into its physical actions but recognises that a person is lord of his acts: he intends them and they are his. Hence it is in order in understanding a person, to look for patterns in his intention/actions sequences as found in the narratives of his actions.

How do I communicate to someone what a person is like? I tell stories about him. This is what the Gospels do in connection with Jesus. They describe the patterns of Jesus' attitudes, intentions, actions, towards men and God: "a skilful storyteller can make a character 'come alive' simply by his narration of events, 'come alive' in a way that no number of straightforward propositional descriptions of the same personality could accomplish .... Moreover, what one knows about the story's central agent is not known by 'inference' from the story. On the contrary, he is known quite directly in and with the story, and recedes from cognitive grasp the more he is abstracted from the story".[14]

When we think about it judgements are being made continually concerning people on the basis of their intention/action. Recently a mother was accused of neglecting her children and they were taken from her into care. This was not based on isolated incidents but as a result of a critical observation of her behaviour over a period of time. On the other hand, if it could have been maintained that while a behaviour pattern was wrong (recent case of stealing) it had a good intention (stealing for children because of lack of money) the judgement would have been different.

The stories told about Jesus (Gospels) were written after the event in which his identity was decisively manifested, i.e. resurrection. This has been seen from the point of view of historical criticism as a disadvantage for it shows that they are testimonies of faith and are overlaid with theological intention. But this may not be such a disadvantage. The Gospels themselves insist that his disciples did not see the full significance of what he did until after his death and it is admitted that people too close to events do not normally understand their intentions. "The larger intention with which a person acts is never fully evident until the action is over — and sometimes not even then. More often than not, it is only the story which others tell about the person after he is gone that reveals the full meaning of his action".[15]

Let us then try to understand the intention/actions of Jesus. It is accepted that he was a charismatic personality so that he was able to get men to follow him unconditionally. His service took priority over every human relationship and every other demand of the world.[16]

His challenge to service was directed not only to the prosperous who held high office in the land but to the poor and outcast. His pattern of behaviour shows him as consorting with sinners and indicated something new and original. The general command of the Old Testament forbade such association on the grounds that it would contaminate the righteous man. Hence this was a source of conflict with the religious leaders.[17]

Again, his healing of leprosy was a new note revealing intense compassion for the sufferer who was outside respectable Jewish society. This violated the ceremonial law since coming into contact with such a disease meant defilement.

Such 'original' behaviour together with an authority which was recognised by both friend and foe produced not only opposition but astonishment. Either his work was 'of the devil' or 'from God'. Of course many followed him because of the 'wonders' that he performed but it appears that Jesus' main intention was not to be followed because of such power but to proclaim the kingdom of God in word and deed.[18]

Teacher, preacher, healer: these appear to be indisputable about the activity of Jesus and they were distinguished by characteristics which set him apart from others who performed similar actions.

Those, for example, who accept that Jesus healed people do not always realise the extent of the claim. With regard to leprosy the Law could do nothing for the leper except protect the rest of the community from him and, according to the rabbis, the healing of leprosy was 'as difficult as the raising of the dead'. Again, the cleansing of leprosy was an expected sign of the arrival of the Messiah.[19]

Further, though exorcisms were performed by other people, it is certainly the intention of Mark to underline that the acts of Jesus in this respect produced such profound astonishment that they were to be considered in a different class.[20]

Again, it is generally accepted that it was the intention of Jesus to teach his disciples to regard the Messiah in a different light from current ideas. The Jewish picture of the kingdom of God was an earthly one and the Messiah would be an earthly king raised up by God to inaugurate it. He would be a glorious figure for whom defeat and suffering would be entirely foreign.[21]

Jesus, however, taught that the Messiah or Son of Man must suffer. Since we are stressing patterns of a consistent nature in the Gospels it can hardly be doubted that this is a constant theme.[22] It starts with the account of the Temptation where worldly power is renounced, emphasised to the disciples at Caesarea Philippi, and realised in the Passion Narrative. Further, the pattern of temptation to resist such suffering is repeated through the agency of the disciples who are seeking worldly power.[23] Again, this stress on suffering is consistent with the pattern of behaviour that refuses to use force to compel belief. Hence Jesus refuses to give a power sign to the Pharisees.[24]

Suffering is connected with doing the will of God. This for Jesus is all important. Even the closest human relationship must not prevent a man doing what he knows to be the will of God.[25] His family err here and try to prevent his activity but those who do the will of God recognise the divine nature of such activity and follow him. This recognition and willingness to follow mean that they are the true brethren of Jesus.[26] Yet the doing of that will involves a struggle even for Jesus and the temptation to turn away from it persists to the end.[27]

Teacher, preacher, healer — and a prophet. The extraordinary nature of his activity is due to his being a spirit-filled prophet in a context of expectation.[28] Such expectation contained the idea that one of the 'old prophets' would return to deliver Israel (Dt. 18 : 15). Here, while it is debatable that Jesus identified himself with the Deuteronomistic concept, it is generally recognised that Jesus interpreted his mission and course of action in accord with latter day prophecy.[29] In particular, he represented himself as ushering in God's time of mercy.[30]

This prophet was to be very special since he would have 'something of God' in his person: God's name was set upon him, i.e. Lord (Adonai, Maran,

41

Kyrios) and he would be fully identified with the cause of God.[31] If Jesus was identified in some way with the 'eschatological prophet' in the days of his flesh then, as Schillebeeckx argues, there is "considerable continuity between the impression that Jesus made during his earthly days and the apparently 'advanced Christology' of the Church's kerygmata or affirmations of belief after his death ..... for such an acknowledgement of Jesus as the eschatological prophet of the nearness of God's kingdom, viewed from the standpoint of the developing tradition, broached a store of synonyms or at any rate associations in which there figure prominently such titles as the Christ, the Kyrios, the Son of God."[32]

In various ways the Gospels stress the 'eschatological' nature of Christ's work. Though these at times reflect later reflections of the Church, they do reflect an older tradition. Mark asks whether or not he is the propheta redivivus, either the revivified John the Baptist or Elijah, Matthew thinks also of Jeremiah in this connection, and Luke has Jesus expounding the great annunciation of the eschatological Christ-prophet at the beginning of his ministry and at the end speaking to the disciples on the road to Emmaus of the eschatological prophet, "who was the one to redeem Israel."[33]

This identification of Jesus based on his extraordinary activity produced two basic reactions: opposition and acceptance. These reactions are confirmed by two historic facts, namely, crucifixion and community.[34]

The distinctive nature of the activity of Jesus as a prophet centred around his proclamation of the kingdom of God as both present and to come. Hence the narrative while concerned with the past in a historical sense, is also existential, i.e. calling men to decision in the present, and eschatological, i.e. the time had arrived when God was going to inaugurate His rule not only here and now but in the last days.[35]

This also relates to the miracle stories in that they are distinctive from parallel stories, both Jewish and pagan, being characteristic of the new age as expressed in Old Testament prophecies.[36]

Jesus was identified with the anointed one of Isaiah 61 who heralded the new age by his works and the proclamation of the kingdom of God. But as we saw in the last chapter, modern theology is inclined to dismiss such eschatology as being the expression of a primitive society. A.E. Harvey is not so sure that such a judgment is correct. Why should we consider the ancient world 'primitive' in accepting an end of the present age when such ideas are not so different from our own. To posit an end is necessary both in fictional stories and in order to make sense of experience. Further, the threat of nuclear war or accident, or ecological disaster foreshadow

42

for us the time of the end; and it is the New Testament promise of a radically different state of affairs in the near future that has given Christianity its power through the centuries. Thus the teaching of Jesus is not so remote as some have asserted. It contained both a combination of teaching which was appropriate to the normal routine and to the exceptional demands of an emergency. The time scale he offered for his predictions was the only one open to him. Indeed, modern-day 'prophecy' in relation to the threat of nuclear war is exactly on a par with this, for only the time scale of a generation can give urgency to the message. His message has power because of 'its promise of a future which is not ideal or utopian, nor a mere variation for the better on what we know already, but is both radically new and able to be envisaged on a human time-scale, "in our generation".[37]

This eschatological sense of mission is sustained for Jesus by his consistent pattern of prayer to God which is witnessed to by the Gospels.[38] Such prayer is by no means a serene experience but marked at times by tears and agony. The latter shows how human the experiences of Jesus were and how dependent he was upon God. But such communion is also distinguished by a familiar mode of address: 'Abba Father' which speaks of the closest intimacy with God. The term was used in a secular sense when the Jewish boy addressed his father and signified for the son the authority and instruction of the father. A failure to obey the father's will was tantamount to rejecting the Torah or Law. Hence with Jesus in his relationship to God it expressed his obedience: 'Not my will, but your will, Father'. This consciousness of intimacy with God is confirmed by his use of 'my Father' (forty-six times in the four Gospels) and his refusal to use the terminology 'our Father'.[39]

This pattern of prayer and consciousness of an intimate relationship with God is generally accepted and seen as the source and ground of Jesus' message as the eschatological prophet. Looking for patterns, as we are doing, there is a connection here with revelation. The 'familial father-concept' appears again in a deeper context in what has been called the Johannine logion in the synoptic gospels: 'I thank thee, Father, Lord of heaven and earth, that thou hast hidden these things from the wise and understanding and revealed them to babes; yea, Father, for such was thy gracious will. All things have been delivered to me by my Father; and no one knows the Son except the Father, and no one knows the Father except the Son and anyone to whom the Son chooses to reveal him. (Mt. 11; 25–27; Lk. 10; 21–22).

Historically, this has been disputed but the substance is very early and has connection with the eschatological messenger and what we shall mention later: 'the Wisdom Christology'. Further it expressed the idea, which is not in dispute, that Jesus had authority from the Father. Moreover, it connects with the use of 'Abba' which we have just noted above for there is the distinction between the Jewish father-formula 'Father, Lord of heaven and earth' and 'Father' (Abba) used absolutely.[40] Hence while the saying may be post-Easter it reflects the pattern we have noticed in the use of 'Abba' and has the important indication that Jesus is the sole mediator of God's revelation and God's agent.

This 'Abba' experience appears to have been the basis of the eschatological hope which Jesus proclaimed in a world which seemed to have lost hope of any real and permanent change taking place. In this too, we see a parallel with our own day. Even John the Baptist accepted as a prophet could only proclaim a message of judgment for his world, but the depth of the religious experience of Jesus convinced him that God's new era had arrived and was intimately connected with his person and work.

So far we have seen the picture emerging of Jesus as teacher, healer, prophet, now we need to consider him as redeemer. Israel had of course the tradition of prophetic martyrdom and Jesus' death can be interpreted in this way. On the other hand the passion narrative reflects the view that salvation is connected with suffering and must take place if mankind is to be delivered. We have noted a pattern of suffering in the sayings of Jesus and this is connected with his doing of the will of God. The story which aptly summaries this pattern is that of the Emmaus Road (Lk. 24; 13–22). Again in the passion narrative His death is portrayed by the Church as in some sense a sacrifice. (14.24)

There are, in short, patterns throughout the Gospels of service, suffering, and doing the will of God even unto death. On the human level this death was caused by opposition to Jesus which was evident from the beginning of his ministry in Galilee and culminated in his death at Jerusalem. Since such opposition was at its worst in Jerusalem it is difficult to argue that Jesus was not aware of the danger of going there.[41]

In the story of the Last Supper the pattern of service is extended unto death. Such a death will benefit 'many' i.e. they enter into a new fellowship or covenant.[42] Jesus was accustomed during his ministry to dine with people of different kinds and it was normal at the final stage to eat a farewell meal with his disciples and to say something about the fate that awaited him so that his disciples might be prepared for it. Even though, the story in its detail reflects the past Easter worship, it does in the older layer of tradition contain the announcement of his imminent death and the prospect of renewed fellowship with them in the kingdom of his Father.[43] Such fellowship is his offer of salvation on the basis that his death is not the end but the pathway to a new hope. The story and the

44

actions which reveal his intention show how he evaluated his death. Hence, though we cannot by the historical method, find without dispute a statement by Jesus which can be taken as a clear evaluation of how he regarded his death, this story which contains the statement regarded as the 'primeval rock of the tradition': 'Truly I say to you, I shall not drink again of the fruit of the vine until that day when I drink it new in the kingdom of God.' (Mk. 14: 2, Lk. 22: 15–18, 1 Cor. 11: 26) points to the renewed fellowship which will materialise through his death. "Such self understanding creates the possibility and lays the foundation of the subsequent interpretation by the Christians."[44]

Yet as the story in Gethsemane shows, though Jesus was determined to follow the will of God as he understood it, the temptation to turn away from that will was brought to an agonising point. Here is an incident which, while the details are in doubt, nevertheless indicates the true humanity of Jesus. But it also reflects the total final obedience to his consciousness of the will of God.

Hence a realistic portrait of Jesus which takes into account the historical critical method has at its bedrock the fact that Jesus was an eschatological prophet who had a consciousness of a depth of relationship with God that we can only imagine. Such a relationship ensured a total obedience to the will of God.

Yet according to his own teaching, as we have seen, Jesus envisaged his followers being called to such a doing of the will of God that would take precedence over every blood relationship. This would knit them into a brotherhood which would be called the Christian Church. Jesus, in doing the will of God totally and fully, would not only be the 'pioneer of the faith' but the inaugurator of the rule of God which had taken place in his ministry, death and resurrection.

It was this unity of will with the Father that entitles us to say that he acted out the role of a Son of God in a sense entirely consonant with Judaism: he was totally obedient to the Father, he revealed the truth which he had learnt from his Father, and he acted as his Father's agent, with the full authority of his Father. But it was only the resurrection which enabled his followers to acknowledge him as *the* Son of God.[45]

Thus Mark reflecting in the light of the resurrection, designates Jesus as the Son of God at the opening of his Gospel, recognised as such in the middle, and called by the term at the end.[46]

Hence Paul says that he was declared Son of God by his resurrection and Matthew extends this backward to the baptism of Jesus and then to his

45

conception and birth. He follows the lead of Paul and identifies Jesus with Wisdom. (Prov. Ch. 8) The writer to the Hebrews combines this Wisdom Christology with the Adam Christology and also expresses a little of the Logos Christology. Basically he sees Christ in Platonic terms as the ideal itself. But it is John 1: 1–18 which makes explicit statement of the doctrine of incarnation: in verse 14 we have 'not only the transition .... from pre-existence to incarnation, but the transition from impersonal personification to actual person'.[47]

All of this was the Christian attempt to express the reality of this person in particular formulations with probably the Wisdom imagery of pre-Christian Judaism being the first formulation.[48]

But the basic foundation was the act of God in Jesus Christ: this was the departure point, not the taking over of a Gnostic redeemer myth which some theologians would assert. Such a point of view could only be established if the Gospel of John was taken as the starting point which could then be interpreted as the myth of the descent of a divine being sent from heaven. Such an interpretation was part and parcel of second century Gnosticism, but the writer of the Fourth Gospel is at pains to refute such an idea with his stress on the humanity of Jesus. Indeed, James Dunn argues that the Logos-Son Christology was 'only an elaboration of the tension between transcendence and immanence, between personal and impersonal, which had always been present in the Jewish conception of God'.[49] As he says, John took a risk of being misunderstood in his bold use of language to interpret the Christ-event to men of his age and it was a measure of his genius that he hazarded so much and yet pulled it off so successfully.[50]

Yet while the Logos or Word concept is valuable when we are thinking of revelation since it speaks of a 'light that lighteth every man that cometh into the world' (Jo. 1) it raises difficulties when the relation of Jesus to the Father and the relation of divinity and humanity in his person are discussed. It tended in the history of the Church to emphasize the subordinate rank of the Logos as a person who proceeded from God in the time sequence and it served to separate the Son's divinity from the historical revelation.[51]

In the picture of Jesus that we have sought to construct from the Synoptic Gospels, the consciousness of Jesus, so far as we can know it, was related to the Father and not to the Logos.

In order to understand this and the person of Jesus more fully it is necessary to consider briefly what Wolfhart Pannenberg says about modern anthropology. He points out that animals have an environment but man has a world.

Animals react to stimuli from their environment in what appears to be a closed system; but man interprets his world and responds to the meaning he finds in it in a more open system. He has an 'openness to the world' (*Weltoffenheit*): this is the basis of man's freedom and his dominion over the world. But man can become self-centred in seeking to fulfil his humanity; if he wishes to preserve his freedom and dominion he needs to exercise faith and hope. These are directed to the future rather than the present or the past. This means more than optimism: it is directing his life towards 'that out of which the future comes to us', i.e. God.

Man has failed in his thinking about God since he has tended to understand Him as the initiator of creation, i.e. the prime mover. Thus history is viewed in a cyclical way with everything returning to its origins. Faith becomes a renunciation of the world and hope is an illusion.

But, as we have seen in the last chapter, God in the Hebrew tradition is the God of the future, transcendent over history, but having the freedom to enter creatively into history.

It was this God that Jesus was 'open to'; and by any criterion he became the greatest personality the world has known. Modern studies confirm the view that isolation and separateness from people can have a devastating effect upon personality. On the other hand dedication to others and living for others eliminates man's natural selfishness. The 'openness' of Jesus to others has emerged in our picture of him and we can maintain that by it he achieved a perfect humanity. But we have also seen that he did it by his complete dedication and obedience to the Father: 'the openness' to the beyond.

Now both the philosopher Hegel and modern studies appear to confirm the view that the essence of a person is to exist in self-dedication to another person. Unity only comes into existence through the process of reciprocal dedication; in this way one person shares in the essence of the other in spite of continuing personal distinctiveness.

How then does the dedication and obedience of Jesus to God differ from other men, i.e. the prophets, saints, etc. It is different because, as we have seen, it had an unrepeatable eschatological character which meant a claim for his person which brought him to the cross. This was retrospectively confirmed by his resurrection. In his arguments for the resurrection Pannenberg, while acknowledging that the resurrection appearances contain many mythical embellishments, argues they have at their core the fact that Jesus did appear to his disciples. He contends that the enemies of Jesus at Jerusalem would have been able immediately to silence the apostles' preaching had the tomb of Jesus been occupied or unknown, but the early Jewish polemic against Christianity always acknowledged that the tomb of Jesus was known and empty.

However, and here we have the crucial point that makes Jesus different from others in their dedication to God; it is the resurrection that confirms that Jesus is the beginning of the final eschatological event. Without such 'a special occasion' it would have been improbable that people adhering to the Jewish tradition could have conceived of Jesus alone as being such an event.

This means that the unity of Jesus with God and the unity of the divinity and humanity in his person resulted from his dedication to God, which when confirmed by the resurrection, enabled the Church to call him 'the Son'.

The actual unification of God and man took place in the course of the temporal existence of Jesus. This we have described in some detail. Hence from the point of view of those who witnessed the earthly life of Jesus they did not see a divine being clothed in human flesh: that would have been Gnosticism which they are at pains to deny. They saw a human being growing in wisdom and knowledge of God and, unless we are to hold the Greek view, this was not an imperfection. As they watched his extra-ordinary works and actions their opinion of him must have changed from day to day but there was growing recognition that here was the unusual and the novel. Yet what he was or the truth about him could not be decided from the viewpoint of their finite present but only by the future which awaited him. In Hebrew tradition the truth was something which happens: it is the future which reveals identity and essence. This differed from the Greek perspective which thought of truth as lying behind something or someone and needed to be uncovered. According to the Hebrew; who someone is, is decided by what he becomes.

Hence it was the resurrection which revealed the truth about Jesus. This demonstrated the Finality of Jesus: the Eschaton towards which all things have their being had appeared in an anticipatory way.

Thus if we move from what we know about Jesus and try and understand what divinity or God is like we get a different understanding from that put forward by the Greek philosophers. They thought of God as static and timeless but Jesus thought of him as active in our time and history. This does not place a limitation upon God. It does upon us for our past is available to us only in memory and the future only in anticipation, but for God the past, present and future are equally and eternally available to Him. He is Lord of history and time; they are freely at His disposal.[52]

Jesus preached not only the kingdom, but the kingdom of God which in some way was present but yet future. Hence since, "His rule and his being are inseparable, God's being is still in process of coming to be."[53] Here is a dynamic in the being of God which is far away from the static nature of the Greek conception. Does this mean a development in God as propounded by process theology? Pannenberg answers in the negative for, "what turns out to be true in the future will then be evident as having been true all along."[54] We can only speak of development in God from the restricted view of our finitude: it does not go beyond the biblical doctrine that in some sense there is a time yet to come when 'God shall be all in all' (1 Cor. 15: 28).[55]

But this key phrase used by Pannenberg helps us too in our thinking about the person of Christ. By his resurrection he did not become the Son of God, but what was declared and confirmed by that event was seen by the writers of this realistic narrative as being true all along. Writing from the point of view of the end of the history of this man which determined his essence and his identity they saw confirmed not only his eschatological message which he had preached but himself as the Eschaton: the beginning of the end of history.

Galloway attempts to make this thought of Pannenberg more clear.[56] There are some attributes which apply to a person in the whole of his extended identity in time. Consider the statement: 'Scotland's best known poet was born on 25 January 1759'. Someone might say, 'That cannot be true for at that date he had not written any poetry'. Such a remark we would not regard seriously except to say that he had missed the 'grammar' of that kind of attribute, for such an attribute applies to the whole life of the man. Hence of Jesus, Pannenberg can write: "the light that falls back on the pre-Easter Jesus from the resurrection involves his person as a whole."[57]

Further, what we have said already, about God and time may be helpful. The whole of time is present to God: God has a real life in time but not as we experience time. It does not limit Him: He is not excluded from the past or the future as we are. Now if time as a whole is present to God then the resurrection of Jesus is compresent with his birth. Hence from the divine perspective what was declared about Jesus after his resurrection, i.e. divinity, was true all along.

Again, in order to grasp this point we need to repeat that the Greek would not view truth in this way. Truth for him, we recall is something hidden under the changing appearance of things, but for the Hebrew truth is something which happens. For the first, an event in time cannot have constitutional force for the eternal essence of a thing, for the second it can.

But truth is always relative to and limited by our finite understanding. In historical studies it is accepted that an eye witness does not see the full implications of the event, only later does its significance become apparent. With regard to the whole of history it will only be at the end that we will know the full truth of what has happened. Jesus in his resurrection is the anticipation of that end of history, hence his resurrection has implications for every event in history.

The early Church saw this very clearly: the resurrection of Jesus is the first fruits of the general resurrection. Without it all their preaching and belief is hopeless: "If Christ be not risen your faith is vain and ye are still in your sins." (1 Cor. 15: 17)

With regard to the person of Christ does this depart from the view laid down by Chalcedon? It departs from the way the doctrine was expressed, not what the doctrine means.

It means that theology is more in line with what philosophy is saying today about persons. We recall that it was argued that what a person becomes is determined by his relations. Hence from our viewpoint Jesus became the Son of God by his relation with God. But, from the viewpoint of God's eternity, God was always one with Jesus, even before his earthly birth. This too stems from the resurrection.[58]

Further, in considering Jesus' unity with God in terms of will, purpose, dedication, we are giving an account of his person which is more in line with our understanding of the world which views it in terms of processes going on rather than a changeless substratum.

But how does this compare with seeing the subject of the person of Jesus Christ as the Son of God. In the fifth century the statement about two natures inhering in one subject (hypostasis) which was put forward by the Council of Chalcedon thought of the subject as the eternal Son of God. This has always raised the objection, apart from its credibility, that it makes the humanity of the man Jesus 'impersonal' for it is taken up into the eternal identity of the Logos or Son (enhypostatic union).[59]

The basic picture of Jesus however, that we have seen emerging from the Synoptic Gospels is that of one who achieves a relationship and communion with the Father that we can scarely understand. It consists in perfect openness to God. There is no record of his communion with a divine Son of God. But as we have noted the resurrection revealed him as the Eschaton: the beginning of the final event. It is "an anticipation of that fullness of being with God which we can conceive of only as the end and fulfilment of history when God shall be all in all," hence we can say, "it is an *eternal* communion within God. God is a being who in his essence is eternally in communion with this man Jesus of Nazareth. In the divine being, and therefore in reality, there never was a time when he was not. He belongs to the essence of the Father."[60] In this way the identity of the man Jesus with the eternal Son of God is conceived in terms which are compatible with his true humanity. The identity is not direct as we have seen in his relationship with the Father as portrayed in the Gospels but indirect and only revealed by the resurrection.

Is it possible, however, to hold an action Christology, i.e. the actions and intentions of Jesus are at the same time the actions and intentions of God, – and yet be true to Chalcedon formula? Put simply the doctrine means: one Person with two natures or substances and the Person is the eternal Son of God.[61] Modern theology argues convincingly that this makes the humanity of Jesus impersonal. Though it could be argued that it means that the humanity did not for a moment exist in and for itself.

However that may be, 'substance', as then used can mean a number of different things: existence, category or status, stuff or material, form, definition, truth. It has the disadvantage not only of suggesting to us some kind of material 'stuff' but also as a 'substratum', i.e. something lying behind. We have noticed already the latter as being the Greek idea of 'the essence' of something. But since 'substance' or 'nature' can, even in its ancient sense, mean so many different things it encourages a liberal interpretation and not a tying down to one particular definition.

Perhaps it might be better to return to a statement by Gregory of Nyssa in which he pointed out that 'Godhead' signifies an operation not a nature. This is very significant when we compare it, not with a static definition of 'nature', but a dynamic one: 'inherent impulses determining character or action.'

If we take this as our clue and consider the biblical statement that God is a spirit we are thinking of the essence of God as a kind of spiritual energy. Add to that the dynamic actions of God throughout biblical history and we have a divine will encountering human wills. Further, God is love and light. Hence we have a spiritual loving will which radiates light. Tertullian saw light as the best illustration of the relation between God and Christ: "Even when the ray is shot forth from the sun, it is still part of the parent mass; the sun will still be in the ray, because it is a ray of the sun – there is no division of substance but merely an extension. Thus Christ is Spirit of Spirit, and God of God, as light is kindled of light."[62]

We are accustomed today to speak of light waves which maintain certain relations with their sources. Hence we might consider Tertullian's ray as a wave motion, a pattern of undulations in space initiated and reiterated by the sun's discharging energy. We might see this in terms of action rather than substance for, "the continuous identity of a ray of light is not that of a piece of substance, like an arm stretched out elastically from the sun, but consists in certain relations holding between certain events. There is identity of wave length throughout the undulations, and there is also a direct causal relationship between the sun as the source of radiation and this particular procession of light waves. When these two conditions are fulfilled we say that the falling of the light waves upon the surface of the earth is part of a single process which began with the solar activity emitting the radiation."[63]

In the case of the relation of Jesus to God both conditions are important. The identity of wave length throughout the light ray is analogous to the Incarnation as an identity of moral pattern between God's intentions, purposes, actions, and those of Jesus; and the direct causal relationship between the sun and the light ray is analogous to the source of the love of God and love of Jesus for the men and women with whom he had to do.[64]

When we consider it carefully the Bible stresses that of all the great virtues such as faith and hope, love is the greatest. Many consider that the famous chapter on love in 1 Corinthians (13), not only excels in demonstrating this but is Paul's portrait of love incarnate: Jesus Christ. However that may be, love is designated as eternal.

Again the other attributes of God could be considered as determined and related to this essence of love. Thus His wrath is an expression of His love since what father is not angry when he sees his children doing things which can harm them? Again, God's power and the use of it is determined by His love and is thus not arbitrary.

Hence we might come nearer to understanding the person of Christ if we thought of God as a loving Subject. Love in order to express itself must have an object and thus we are moving in the area of Trinitarian thought. If God is love then love finds itself in the other by emptying Himself, yet retaining His identity as subject.[65]

Both the Trinity and Christology can be thought of in terms of relations. The Trinity could consist of relations which penetrate and interpenetrate one another and the same could apply to the divinity and humanity of Christ for the infinite is not excluded by the finite but includes it. Otherwise the existence of the finite would function as a boundary reducing the 'infinite' to finitude. These could overlap, interpenetrate, and be two and one at the same time.[66]

Love reveals not only itself to the other (self-revelation) but fully dedicates itself to the other. Such self dedication is, according to Hegel, the essence of a person. If he is right, then we can view Christology in terms of a reciprocal relationship. Jesus, as we noted, dedicated himself to the Father and the Father, as presented by this realistic narrative, responded a number of times with the words: "This is my beloved Son ..."[67] Such dedication of Jesus, as the eschatological prophet, was confirmed by the resurrection which identified him with the essence of God. But we also noted in constructing our portrait of Jesus from the Synoptic Gospels that differentiation from God was an element in the life of Jesus, i.e. he prayed to Him, trusted in Him. relied upon Him etc. Hence if we move from our understanding of Jesus to understand what God is like, then differentiation belongs to the essence of God.

Then the unity of the Trinity is a unity of reciprocal self-dedication which is the result of reciprocal relations. All is made possible because the essence of God is love.[68]

We have sought to define a person in relational terms and it can be argued that this was the way Chalcedon saw it. Certainly the real complication entered in when Boethius later put forward the definition of person as "an individual substance of rational nature", i.e. tends to make person equal nature, so that we could have the idea of two persons in Christ. It was noteworthy that Duns Scotus and Richard St. Victor in the 12th and 13th centuries rejected such a definition and returned to the relational view of person.

Thus we can express the relation of the divinity and humanity in two ways:

a) The finite consciousness of Jesus was related to the Son of God in such a way that true humanity emerged. Such a relationship did not make the humanity impersonal it enhanced it for, "God's close proximity does not absorb the creature but makes it more independent."[69]

b) The finite consciousness of Jesus was related to the Father in such a way that *true* humanity emerged. Again, the humanity does not become impersonal.

Chalcedon is reflected in (a), while modern German theology is represented by (b). The pre-existence of Jesus as the eternal Son of God is stressed by Chalcedon by the use of that term, but we can also, as we have seen, reflect the same idea, on the basis of the difference between God's time and ours. With our view of time we think of Jesus Christ as existing from his birth at Nazareth but time is compresent with God, hence from his perspective Jesus Christ is from all eternity.

This way of expressing Christology, though it makes Jesus Christ the centre of the person, upholds the main concern of the Chalcedon definition. It has the advantage of resolving the duality which occurs in the use of the 'Son of God' terminology in connection with the man, Jesus; while still stressing as Chalcedon did, the uniqueness of his person and his unity with God.

Modern English theology, however, fears that such uniqueness is unacceptable in a secular and pluralistic world. How real these fears are will be examined in our final chapter.

CHAPTER 5

Pluralism and Secularisation

As we have noted, English theology has drawn attention to the questions raised for Christianity by the current secular and pluralistic society. There are of course different definitions of secularisation and various reasons for its rise but we have noted that aspect which poses scientific and philosophical questions for the traditional doctrine of the Incarnation.

We shall return to this problem later in the present chapter but first of all we want to consider the questions posed by a pluralistic society. Increasing contact with, and knowledge of, other religions has drawn a variety of responses from Christian sources.[1]

The writing of the mythographers is one such reaction which recognises that the traditional doctrine of the Incarnation is an obstacle to a future global theology.[2] Hence, as we have seen, they consider that the way forward is to see such doctrine as a myth. However, they are reluctant to embrace the Unitarian position and in their understanding of Jesus speak at times of him in such elevated terms that they have been accused of Arianism.[3]

However that may be, it is clear that to speak of Jesus as 'Final' (Young) or as presenting the 'absolute claim of God' (Hick) would not be acceptable to religions such as Islam which, while considering him a prophet, think Mohammed to be *the* prophet.[4]

It is John Hick, however, who has paid most attention to the relation between Christianity and other religions and we need to consider his position before attempting to establish our own. Hick believes that religious diversities derive from geographical isolation which explains why the encounter with the same God is so varied. He was given various Names and His Actions understood in different doctrinal formulae. Just as we once erred in thinking of the earth as the centre of the universe with all the planets revolving around it so we must avoid the mistake of thinking of Christ as the centre of the revelation of God.

But, as Kenneth Cragg points out, the earth is the centre for us despite our increasing knowledge of other planets and similarly Christ remains the centre for the Christian. Further, Hick's argument which regards religious diversities as deriving from geographical isolation does not take into account that Judaism/Christianity, Christianity/Islam, perhaps even Buddhism/Christianity, have been interpenetrating, interacting spheres of faith through much of their history and hardly any of them are explicable without reference to another. "Traditional attitudes may long have been formed in ignorance. But they are not dispelled only by familiarity. Most important of all, Christian faith in Christ as 'Son of God' has first been faith in a historic actuality in order to be, also as Hick rightly stresses, the Christian's proceeding upon his image of God."[5]

In more recent times, Hick has gone further in recognising the validity of other religions. At a Jewish/Christian/Muslim conference in Birmingham 1981, he intimated that he regarded the Incarnation as, "a fusion of divine grace and creaturely freedom", of which the life of Jesus Christ was a primary example, but which occurs in "all authentic human response and obedience to God". Christians who, "feel impelled to claim superiority for their own tradition", can still do so by saying that such fusion of the divine and the human was most perfectly exemplified in Jesus; but this sense of superiority is different from the way in which Christians have traditionally understood the superiority of their religion in that it does not stand in the way of their recognizing that a fusion of the divine and the human also lies at the basis of Judaism and Islam and that these religions too enable man to make an authentic response to God. Hick, however, showed reservations even about this relative type of superiority of Christianity, since he thought that it can only be judged on the basis of a sufficiently complete knowledge of the historical Jesus, a knowledge that we do not possess.[6]

We note that it was just this latter difficulty that we sought to overcome in Chapters Two and Four by regarding the evidence at our disposal as realistic narrative.

However, the thought of Hick appears to be moving from what he and other mythographers held, namely, that God was supremely encountered in Jesus, to contending that God is equally encountered in all religions. We can put this another way. All religions use mythological discourse which evoke an appropriate response to the sources of salvation within their tradition. The myths thus developed are equally true, in that they all evoke appropriate attitudes. To treat them as competing theories is to misunderstand their mythological character: "They are more like different art forms, each of which is at home in a different culture, than like rival scientific hypotheses."[7]

If this is the case, however, we might wonder why Christianity produced a discourse which led to the doctrine of the Incarnation whereas other religions did not. The nearest parallel is the avatar concept in Hinduism but here there are many incarnations. Indeed the Hindu cannot understand why Christianity focusses on one particular person.

Again, what the mythographers are saying about the relation of Christianity to other religions is based upon their view of the divine action. Divine acts do not take place 'between worldly occurrences' (gaps left by natural events) but in them (hidden) which does not affect the closed web of cause and effect. The 'miraculous' is rejected as a solution but the idea of 'experiencing as' (a sense of life as purposive in response to the prior purposive activity of God towards man) is acceptable.[8]

The point being made here is that God has always been in touch with his world and does not need to intervene directly in the sense of breaking into the natural. He expresses Himself through the creation and by special events in history. 'Special' really means being more fully expressed. If the question is pressed: What is special? The answer is in terms of response. Some people by virtue of their personality and situation are more fully responsive to the divine action than others; in the case, however, of Jesus the response was total.

There are difficulties here. It is true that divine action is based upon a general human response or what we call religious experience. But while the religious experience of mankind testifies to such a situation there are many people who equally testify to no experience of such action. Moreover, religious experience can be explained in purely humanistic and secular terms, eg. Freud and other materialists.

Further, there is a problem about the relation of religion based on human experience and special events: "... One wonders whether there is not a measure of inconsistency between the claim that a truth is, on the one hand based on human experience generally but, on the other hand, brought home very potently by certain events in history. If it is based on human experience why is it not brought home potently by such experience? Conversely, if it is brought home very potently by certain events, might it not be said to be based on these events?"[9]

However that may be, the Bible appears to speak of a general revelation (Ps. 19. 1–4, Rom. 1. 19–20) and this has been much debated in recent times.[10]   But the focus of the religions of Israel, Christianity, Islam, Buddhism is not on this, but on a particular people and events. Thus the prophet plays the leading role in Israel and Islam, and the Buddha in Buddhism. With regard to Jesus a clear distinction is made between God speaking through the prophets and His Son (Hebrews 1 : 1). 'Particularity', as we argued in Chapter Three, has a major role in Christianity and now we see it emerging in other Faiths.

It is significant that current English theology has moved to an emphasis on God rather than Christ whereas the recent 'death of God' theology stressed the central role of Christ. Thus Hick came to 'the realisation that it is God who is at the centre, and that all religions of mankind, including our own revolve around him."[11] Again, other writers in England have made much use of the Spirit in connection with the Incarnation.[12] Here it is tempting to recall certain theology of the nineteenth century which ended in Unitarianism having passed through various phases of revelation which moved from God to Jesus and then to the Spirit.[13]

But if we accept Hick's position this does not mean that we will know God. Even if we effect a union of all religions we must still remain agnostic about God. He writes: "May it not be that the different concepts of God, as Jaweh, Allah, Krishna, Param Atma, Holy Trinity and so on; and like- wise the different concepts of the hidden structure of reality, as the eternal emanation of Brahman or as an immense cosmic process culminating in Nirvana, are all images of the divine, each expressing some aspect or range of aspects and yet none by itself fully and exhaustively corresponding to the infinite nature of the ultimate reality?"[14]

D.B. Forrester's comment on this is worth noting: "Hick believes, it appears, that all religions in their 'experiential roots' are in contact with the same ultimate reality, but that only the differences in the understanding of that reality are culturally determined 'secondary, human, historical develop- ments'. One wonders whether perhaps he has not capitulated to a relativism which is unlikely to be acceptable to committed believers except for Vedantic Hindus."[15]

There seems to be in the Hick proposal an attempt to conflate religions but this is generally accepted as not possible. A better way would be to check and develop each religion as accurately as possible, "and lay it charitably and boldly alongside other projections which also claim to guide man in his pilgrimage."[16] This must be done in openness and affection but in the conviction that Christianity has something distinctive to offer and to share with other Faiths.

Hick's viewpoint resembles the Hindu perspective rather than the Christian. For the Hindu all religions point ultimately to the one Truth. They are all 'true' in some way for both Christ and Krishna are different manifestations of the one God.

Arguments against this viewpoint are: a movement, religious or otherwise, which does not have a distinctive message tends to wither; the focus in various religions is different, i.e. Christ in Christianity, Mohammed in Islam, Buddha in Buddhism etc; there is incompatibility between religious truth claims and divergence in practice-claims.[17]

Further, it is questionable whether we can proceed on the belief that there is a common core of religious experience in all religions. N. Smart writes: "I do not wish to argue the point here; but my own view is that there is no common core, but rather that there are different sorts of religious experience which recur in different traditions, though not universally. From a phenomenological point of view it is not possible to base the judgement that all religions point to the same truth upon religious experience."[18]

Our position concerning Christ gives him a universal and cosmic role which arises out of the uniqueness of his relation with God being confirmed by the resurrection. This is derived from the portrait of Jesus based on the Synoptic Gospels, but it is also the view of the letters of the Apostle Paul (Col. 1. 15—17, Eph. 1. 9—10). How can such a view enter into dialogue with other religions?

One of the most fruitful concepts used by the writer of the Fourth Gospel was the Logos. The early Church called this principle 'spermaticos' which like a seed is and was everywhere in the world, since the beginning of the world and of mankind. Thus revelation and salvation were always operating in history even before the embodiment of the Logos in Jesus; and this was continued by the power of the Logos under the guidance of the Spirit. Hence we can speak of the universality of Christianity.[19]

It might be better, however, to use the term 'Christ' instead of Logos for we have noted how in the use of the concept by the early Church Fathers it had at times the overtones of 'a secondary god'. Jesus was the name applied to many people during the first century and of these persons one was called Christ, meaning the Anointed One. This idea is even older than the Old Testament and comes probably from Egypt, out of the royal house, and from there went to Israel. It is a very old symbol with a long history.[20]

In addition to it being used in connection with the empirical manifestation of God in Jesus it was the term preferred by Paul (Eph. i. 4; Phil. 2.5 etc) and it appears in the Synoptic Gospels from which we have drawn our portrait.

This 'Light' of salvation then has both a particular and universal revelation. However, when we read the literature of inter-faith dialogue, the impression often arises that religions are contending with one another for possession of revelation as related to their individual founders. But there is a strain of biblical teaching which relates the general revelation to man as such. Thus the writer of the Fourth Gospel speaks of the 'light that lighteth every *man* that cometh into the world (Jo. 19). Paul speaks of the revelation of God being given to men" (Ro. 1. 19) and the writer to the Hebrews acknowledges that God has spoken in "many and various ways by the prophets." (Heb. 1. 1)

The response however has not been good and even when the light of Christ has been given, men have turned away from it. The Church is the people of the New Covenant yet it cannot be said that the visible Church in general lived up to that Covenant. Hence theologians have spoken of 'the invisible' Church: the people who have really held to the Covenant. This is paralleled by the doctrine of 'the remnant' in the Old Testament whose calling was one of witness and responsibility. It did not give them a feeling of superiority but to light a beacon for the world.

Since all men have been created in Christ and He has died for all men it follows that He, in ways unknown to us, is at work among men everywhere, not only in what we call the great religions of the world but in secular movements such as communism, secularism, nationalism. Thus a sociologist can see 'signals of transcendence' in *man*, as indicated by his experience of trust and being trusted, which happens in the parent/child world; in play and games as giving us an angle on ourselves beyond ourselves; in humour where the comic somehow liberates us from the prison of the world; in the dimension of hope by which man transcends where he is in a sense of where, or how, he might be. All of these he calls 'divine signals in reality".[21]

Even Karl Barth who in earlier writings was so uncompromising in his view of God's self-revelation in Jesus Christ has admitted in his later work that there are other witnesses to the truth of Christ outside the Church. He speaks of these lights in the world which are refractions of the light of

Christ so that in them the community of Christ recognises "with joy something of its own proper message" or "being forced to recognise this with
shame because by (these other voices) it is shown and made to realise the
omissions and truncations of its own message".[22]

This latter point of Barth's is important for it could be interpreted as the
claim of other religions and secular movements as judging Christianity.
The protest of Mohammed, for example, against the irreligious quality of
life in Mecca is paralleled by the condemnation of the religion of his day
by Jesus. Again, when Christianity has been reduced to a mainly private
affair of an individual and his communion with God, which happened in
various religious movements following the Reformation of the 16th century,
then we may be at liberty in seeing the Spirit of Christ more active in the
inspiration given to their culture of Islam and Buddhism. Further, communism and secularism with their protest concerning the ills of society
have at times more of that Spirit than that aspect of Christianity which
occupied itself solely with pietism.

The converse of course is true. Christianity's experience of the spirit of
Christ will mean that it will give as well as receive in the dialogue with
other Faiths. Christian ideas, values, principles have affected and will affect
members of other religions when they are really lived out in that environment. It would appear that when Christianity first emerged in the Roman
Empire they were known as people of 'the way'. If this is so, it is significant
that people are inclined to enquire about beliefs after they have seen a
particular way of life lived amongst them.

Encounter with Hinduism which is inclined to think 'unhistorically' may
be altered by the Christian's experience of history as reality; encounter with
Islam which is inclined to a fatalistic attitude may induce the Christian's
belief that the world can be changed and people have a responsibility for
changing it.[23]

But perhaps the most important change in the attitude of Christianity
today is that it will judge itself not only in the light of that which it stands
for, namely "the decisive self-manifestation in human history of the source
and aim of all being" but also the presence of that Christ in the depths of
every faith.[24]

If it should be argued at this point that we are asserting an absolute claim
for Christ it is worth recalling that other religions also make such assertions.
This is one thing that they have in common! It is unlikely, therefore, that
such religions will easily retract their categorical assertions for the sake of
a quick reconciliation. In dialogue they may be reformulated but such

reformulation is unlikely to dilute the content of the experience which it interprets.[25]

Having considered the problem of pluralism,[26] we need at this point to pay attention to that aspect of secularisation which permeates the thinking of the mythographers namely that the Incarnation can be seen as part of the pre-modern or pre-scientific way of viewing the world that was prior to the rise of modern western scientific thought. This means that the New Testament community was culturally conditioned and that what they wrote was relative both to time and place. Hence the older interpretation of Jesus was appropriate for the early centuries and the deification of Jesus was inevitable if his message was to spread and survive.[27]

In other words they created doctrines and believed things which would be impossible for us today. This is a very serious challenge for it places them in the category of the naive and credulous.

We have noted before however that this was not so. When a 'miracle' is reported to them for example it is greeted with scepticism: "Never since the world began has it been heard that anyone opened the eyes of a man born blind."[28] Again, when the resurrection is reported one of them refuses to accept the witness until empirical evidence is presented to him.[29]

Further, we cannot rule out events happening because they are foreign to our experience. It was the custom in the ancient world for Greeks and Romans to expose their new-born children in order to control the numbers of the population. This is so foreign to our experience that we could rule out the report as improbable but it is none the less true.[30]

However, it is alleged that the current scientific world view is the big obstacle to our acceptance of divine intervention by means of an Incarnation. We have noted this way of thinking in chapter four and have argued that nineteenth century science was more certain of what 'reality' was than our age. Hence the popular views of David Friedrich Strauss concerning the naive and mythological writers of the New Testament carried much more force than the present arguments of the mythographers. Today, as we have seen, science is not so sure about a 'world view' for the concepts that comprise contemporary categorical frame works are in a state of flux: "we are confronted by paradoxes that have stubbornly resisted all efforts at resolution and by mythological processes without empirical validation but whose function is to link together observable phenomena into some kind of connected whole. It has become commonplace for scientists to emphasise the role of imagination and creativity in science even to the point of saying that physics is a kind of poetry."[31] In such a climate of scientific opinion it is somewhat surprising to find the mythographers embarrassed by the apparent paradoxes and illogicality of Christian teaching.

Here Wittgenstein's observation is pertinent to those who think that they know what the proper 'world view' is: When we declare some set of propositions to be necessary to say how the world is, this only means that we have failed to think of an alternative.

What is more realistic is to recognise that "we live in a culture that is pluralistic with respect to world views, so that atheism, agnosticism, and theism all have a measure of support. And within these world views the role of science is both complex and disputed. To claim that science of itself constitutes a world view is not at all clear, while to claim that science gives definite support to one particular world view is a matter of deep dispute."[32]

There is no doubt however that both scientifically and technologically we are far in advance of the thinking of the first century. But it is more difficult to argue that we are more spiritually advanced than they were. Indeed the mythographers recognise that Jesus is a moral ideal worthy of emulation. Further, in matters such as the knowledge of God we may be cognitively inferior to those in earlier periods of our history. If our portrait of Jesus is adequate then we know that he based his actions on the knowledge of God gained through prayer. Such knowledge achieved a prophetic breakthrough which makes our knowledge of God look meagre.

It is a fallacy to argue from the premise that modern consciousness is secularised to the conclusion that modern consciousness is epistemologically superior to the New Testament writers. Thus Peter Berger, commenting on Bultmann's belief that modern electricity and radio-users have an epistemological superiority over the New Testament writers, opposes his contention that they have unquestioned cognitive superiority over such spiritual experts as the apostle Paul.[33]

It is one thing to argue that we cannot accept what they say because they held a scientific view of the world that involved a three-storey conception but quite another that we rule out what they write about spirits and miracles. Bultman puts them altogether. Yet we noted in a previous chapter how extensive psychical research has become and controversy about occult phenomena and the demonic could also be documented. "We can envisage as much if not more debate about miracles, as is suggested by the continuation of scholarly debate on this issue."[34]

Closely related to this view of the credulity of the New Testament writers is the idea that it was the product of its environment and not binding on us today. This comes through with particular reference to the Incarnation.

Here the old debate comes to the fore: Does the environment create the religion or does the religious founder bring something which is new and novel. Here it is not necessary to dwell on the response of the first century environment to Christianity for we have already noted that what the early apostles were saying, especially in connection with the resurrection of Jesus, ran counter to the belief both of Jew and Greek. Certainly, the New Testament writers believed that in Jesus they had the novel. Saviours had emerged in Judaism before but had not had the impact of Jesus: He was the eschatological figure, the One who through his death and resurrection had inaugurated a new age. Hence the unique claim which even Islam does not make, for Mohammed appears to have regarded himself as standing in the tradition of the earlier prophets.[35]

It is one thing to say that the environment was favourable for the rise of a religion such as Christianity it is another thing to argue that environmental ideas caused it. Further, at times favourable environments have been present for the development of a religion but no world wide religion such as Christianity has arisen. The mythographers, perhaps, have paid too much attention to the impact of the Greek environment upon Christianity and not enough to its roots in Hebrew thought. Francis Young admits, however, that it was not a matter of one or two simple borrowings, but a 'tangled mass' of ideas; and even if this could be fully demonstrated the natural outcome would be a docetic Christ which is explicitly opposed by the New Testament writers. Christianity, in short, refused "to stray too far from the historical reality of Jesus of Nazareth."[36]

To reject the doctrine of the Incarnation then, either on the basis of being caused by the environment of the time or as being too improbable for modern consciousness to accept, rests on dubious grounds. Perhaps theologians should pay more attention to what sociologists are saying about our secular society before making it the criterion of what we should believe. It would appear that when the mythographers have to make a decision between what the New Testament writers say and what modernity asserts they must accept the latter and not the former.

Yet a recent writer complains that theologians do not substantiate what they assert about modern society and indeed are playing the role of 'amateur sociologists'. He points out that one leading sociologist even goes so far as to deny that we have a pluralist society. More likely, however, is his verdict that what we have today is ambiguity: there are processes of both secularisation and de-secularisation apparent within our contemporary society and possibly within all societies. Again, what goes on among the academic community differs from the 'global consciousness' but even in our institutions of higher learning positivism and behaviourism have not generally been victorious.[37]

Christianity, however, will always have to face the questions posed by current thought. It cannot avoid them or consider them irrelevant. Hence the thinking of the mythographers has been very useful in seriously seeking a way to express the significance of Christ in our modern world. Further, Christianity will have to be as open as possible in its dialogue with other Faiths, this too was worth emphasising by John Hick, who has given time and attention to this problem.

But the uniqueness of Christ as we have tried to express it does not set limits to God's activity in the world. It emphasises that co-operation and co-existence can exist in face of doctrinal differences but it precludes a view of Christ which makes relative in order to. achieve a quick reconciliation. Further, such uniqueness of Christ provides a hope, even if it is an eschatological one, that the future (the unknown quality of which is one of the limits of secularisation) will not be so dark as some of the scientific apocalypses envisage.

APPENDIX 1

Past controversies and the present problem

It is the purpose of this appendix to show that this recent opposition to the doctrine of the Incarnation is the latest phase of an opposition that has been perennial in the history of the Church.

It is usual to illustrate this point by going back to the early centuries of the Church and dealing with the Arian controversy or to show from a description of the radical left wing of the Reformation, i.e. anti-Trinitarians, their opposition to the deity of Christ.

We choose, however, to establish parallels with the current controversy by particular reference to the centuries immediately preceding our own for the claim of the mythographers is that the advance of scientific thinking has brought a new dimension to the debate. The nineteenth century witnessed the conflict between science and religion with the publication of Darwin's *Origin of the Species* (1859) and led many theologians both of the liberal and unitarian tradition to look for a new authority for their theology rather than the Bible which was under attack. Some found this in reason, others in conscience, and some in feeling, etc. But before the nineteenth century, the general tendency of Unitarians was to see themselves as true followers of the Reformers for they rejected human creeds and confessions and tried to return to the Bible itself. Thus, they escaped as they thought, the corruptions of the primitive faith which had taken place in the early centuries of Christianity due largely to the work of the Greek philosophers.

We shall consider first of all, the opposition to creeds and confessions from the seventeenth century based on the principle that no authority had the right to compel assent to such documents. This was contrary to the right of private judgment. Gradually, however, this opposition to creeds based on a man's right to search the scripture for himself and arrive at a personal belief became a protest against the doctrines which the creeds and confessions contained.

From the seventeenth century onwards the clarion cry of the man who refused to subscribe to creeds and confessions was: "The Bible, the Bible only is the religion of Protestants."[1]

No document drawn up by men is to be put in the place of that which is the supreme rule of faith and practice. Writers and preachers pleaded for the liberty of Bible reading, the right of private judgment, and the proper use of conscience in matters of faith.

They argued most strongly against the practice of the Church of imposing articles of faith upon its members which were not expressed in the words of scripture, and in charging men with heresy who refused to subscribe to her formulas. A noble array of names confronts the student of the seventeenth century as he seeks light on the revolt against creeds: Chillingworth, Milton, Stillingfleet, Locke, Taylor, and others. But in addition to their protest against creeds as such, some of them could hardly be called 'orthodox' in their doctrinal position.

Hearnshaw believes that Milton was thinking of the Assembly of Divines at Westminster when he wrote in *Paradise Lost:*[2]

> "Others apart sat upon a hill retired
> In thoughts more elevate and reasoned high
> Of Providence, Fore-knowledge, Will and Fate-
> Fixed Fate, Freewill, Foreknowledge absolute,
> And found no end in wandering mazes lost."

Milton appears to have passed from Puritan orthodoxy to Sabellianism (God in three modes of revelation rather than being) and then to Arianism (Christ regarded as the head of an hierarchy of angels). In his *Treatise on Christian Doctrine* he puts forward an Arian view of Christ as begotten before the world but not from all eternity.[3] God is the source of all his power and knowledge. Since the Father is the sole Deity, he could not communicate his essence to another. The Father alone is self-existent and any being which is not cannot be God; Christ therefore is the first of the creation of God. The Holy Spirit must be inferior to both Father and Son for he is both promised, sent, and given. This follows the rule that the one sent is inferior to the sender. Milton also bases predestination on foreknowledge and denies the doctrine of reprobation; but he takes the side of Calvin on the point of original sin and the atonement.

John Locke (1632–1704) too found himself in debate with the orthodoxy of his day.[4] He denied the doctrine of ideas and principles innate in the mind, and based all knowledge on experience. Man gains knowledge from the impressions of the senses and the reflections of the mind on what it perceives. The mind, in fact, is like a blank sheet of paper.[5]

This philosophic position reflected the view of reality which had emerged in science. Galileo had argued that for a scientist the most important features of any situation were those that could be weighed and measured. Weight, size, number, etc. are the essential components of any substance. This corresponds to the primary qualities in Locke, whereas colour, smell, feeling, etc. are the secondary qualities.[6] The measurable had become the real. Newton provided the universal principle of gravitation to account for the movement of all bodies: the stars in their courses and the apple that falls from the tree both move according to the same rules.[7] Science dealt with masses or atoms moving in space according to mathematical laws: matter in motion was reality, the whole was a great machine. In his *Essay concerning Human Understanding* (1960) Locke said that he only needed to know the position and motion of the bits and pieces that constituted rhubarb and opium and he would then be able to predict that rhubarb would purge and opium would make a man sleep. In other words, all we need is the position and motion of anything to predict its future.[8]

The conclusion could only be a universe consisting entirely of mechanical bodies that interacted with one another. The impact of bodies on our nervous system gave rise to 'ideas' in the mind about these bodies. What we are directly aware of are the 'ideas'.[9] This 'billiard-ball' picture of the universe really meant that there was nothing left for God to do once he had started the machine going. He became more and more remote, and Locke's philosophical writings led directly to deism. His empiricism drew much of its inspiration from the importance of experiment and observation in Newtonian science.[10]

Both Newton and Locke, however, found room for the existence of God. Since Newton was unable to account for the precise orbs of the planets in terms of his mechanics, he thought that God personally intervened when they went off their paths. The universe, like a self-winding clock, ran very well on the whole; but it could get out of time, hence it was necessary for God to return to regulate it. It was a limited role and later thinkers were quite willing to dispense with it altogether.[11]

Locke was quite sure that the works of nature gave sufficient evidence for the existence of a Deity, and this provides the basis of a rational proof of his existence. He also, as we will see, left the door open for revelation in his idea of Jesus as the Messiah. But before considering this, we note that in his books *The Reasonableness of Christianity as Delivered in the Scriptures* (1695), he denied the doctrine of Original Sin. What Adam lost by his fall was simply bliss and immortality; and the sentence of death pronounced on mankind because of Adam's sin is to be understood as referring to the death of the body only. Death here means neither eternal misery, nor the corruption of human nature in the posterity of Adam. Every man shall bear his own sin.

Jesus Christ by his resurrection restores all mankind to eternal life. The only belief required is that Jesus is the Messiah. This was the fundamental article of the primitive Church, according to the Gospels and the Acts. As Christ recovered for man the gift of immortality which has been lost, God has rewarded him by assigning to him, as Messiah, an everlasting Kingdom. Those who accept Jesus as the Messiah, repent of their sins, and sincerely seek to obey the divine law, shall receive immortality.

Locke distinguished between one part of the New Testament and another. He did not remain attached to the traditional interpretation which treated each part on the same level, but noticed everywhere advance, development, and different shades of doctrinal opinion. He speaks of the 'occasional' character of the Epistles. Much of them was written by way of accommodation of the Christian truth to the special needs of the readers, and has little permanent value. It is not in the Epistles that we learn the fundamental truths of Christianity, but in the preaching of Christ and his Apostles.[12]

Here Locke was the forerunner of the principle of modern theology which sees a doctrinal development in the apprehension of the New Testament writers and draws a distinction between the canonical books. Certainly Locke, both as a theologian and a biblical critic was the model of the older school of English Unitarianism.[13] His emphasis, too, on reason's capacity to test revelation was to have far-reaching results. Locke was convinced that reason must confirm whether revelation was in conformity with self-evident truths or proceeded from the proper inspired source. If not, it must be declared false.[14]

An important event occurred in the middle of the seventeenth century with the passing of the Act of Uniformity (1662). Many ministers had entered the Church without episcopal ordination or subscription to the *Thirty-Nine Articles*. They were now required to submit to re-ordination, subscription to the Book of Common Prayer, take the oath of Canonical Obedience, renounce the Solemn League and Covenant, and promise never to take up arms against the King. More than two thousand of them preferred to vacate their livings rather than subscribe. How they continued to live is a mystery, for they were forbidden to do practically anything. Some went to America, others were imprisoned for preaching, and those who were not banished from the country had to maintain their families on less than £10 a year.

The eighteenth century, however, had hardly dawned when the defenders of creeds were dealt another blow by the publication of a book which was destined to become 'the fountainhead of the so-called Arian views'.[15] This was Samuel Clarke's famous work *The Scripture Doctrine of the Trinity,* published in 1712. Clarke taught that there were three divine persons, but the Father alone was self-existent, underived, and independent.[16] He was supreme and the only object of worship; no one else had the right to be called God.

Although the Son and the Spirit were divine persons, they were not divine in the same sense as the Father, since He was self-existent. They only existed as an act of free choice on his part. The Son was subordinate to the Father, and the Spirit subordinate to both Father and Son. He believed that the Son and the Spirit existed from the beginning, but was not willing to speculate on their generation. Clarke would not be drawn into admitting that there was a time when the Son was not, because that was to be presumptuous above what was written in scripture.[17] He could not therefore be rightly called an Arian: Semi-Arian is a better designation of his position. Yet his book caused so much controversy that it gave great impetus to Arianism in the eighteenth century and had much to do with the opposition to the doctrine of the Trinity which was evident during this period. This opposition culminated in the debates which took place on the 24th February 1718, in the Salters' Hall, London. Here subscription to the traditional doctrine of the Trinity was rejected by fifty-seven votes to fifty-three.[18]

On theological questions distinct from the Trinity much damage was done to credal formulations of such doctrines as Original Sin and the Atonement by John Taylor (1694–1761). Alexander Gordon reports that a worthy minister in Ireland begged that none of his hearers would read Taylor's book on Original Sin (1740), 'for it is a bad book, and a dangerous book, and a heretical book; and, what is worse than all the book is unanswerable!'[19] Taylor was an Arian and held the divinity chair at Warrington Academy from 1757. Apart from his attack on Original Sin, he taught that Christ's death was not a satisfaction to divine justice, nor his suffering a vicarious punishment.

70

Taylor was ably supported by Richard Price (1723–90), another Arian, who denied the Trinity, the two natures of Christ, Original Sin, satisfactory Atonement and Predestination.[20] His sermons were published in both England (1787) and Ireland (1819) and did much to unsettle the established orthodoxy.

Scotland did not escape all this opposition to creeds which was taking place at this time in England. Three years after the publication of Samuel Clarke's book on the Trinity, the Professor of Divinity of Glasgow, John Simson (1668–1740), was before the Assembly for heresy. At his trial in 1715, he was charged with teaching Arminianism, and a committee on purity of doctrine was appointed to investigate the charge.

Its report was not given in till 1717. Simson had admitted using questionable modes of expression but had declared that he had never intended to deviate from the teaching of the Church's Confession. He was therefore acquitted with a warning 'not to attribute too much to natural reason and the power of corrupt nature to the disparagement of revelation and efficacious free grace'.[21]

Instead of silencing Simson, this appears to have had the opposite effect, for in a short time he was before the Assembly again, and this time on a charge of Arianism. He was reported to be repeating Clarke's views to his students, denying the independence and necessary existence of the Son and the numerical oneness of the Trinity.[22] This caused a great debate in the Assembly of 1728, 'ranging over the most abstruse points of Trinitarian theology and the canon law affecting heretics'.[23] Simson denied that he held opinions contrary to the *Westminster Confession of Faith,* but admitted that he had used certain ambiguous phrases in connection with it. The Assembly of 1729 decided to suspend him indefinitely from teaching, without deposing or depriving him of his chair.

One of Simson's students was the famous Francis Hutcheson (1694–1746), who imbibed his ideas and expounded them to his friends in his native Ireland. Hutcheson became professor of Philosophy at Glasgow in 1730, and 'the Apostle of the Enlightenment in Scotland'.[24] Hutcheson was, in due course, charged with two heresies: (i) that the standard of moral goodness was the promotion of the happiness of others, and (ii) that we could have a knowledge of good and evil without a knowledge of God. The case, however, did not get any further than the Presbytery of Glasgow. It was Hutcheson, as J.H.S. Burleigh points out, who by judicious wire-pulling secured the appointment of William Leechman, minister of Beith, Ayrshire, to the Glasgow chair of Divinity in 1743. Leechman, he believed, would 'put a new face upon Theology in Scotland'. Burleigh quotes

71

Alexander Carlyle who attended Leechman's class in 1743—4 to the effect that though neither Hutcheson nor Leechman taught heresy, 'Yet they opened and enlarged the minds of the students, which soon gave them a turn for free enquiry, the result of which was candour and liberality of sentiment'.[25]

This free enquiry was spreading far and wide. Here we note its effects in the nineteenth century in America, England, and the Continent of Europe. When Francis Hutcheson was lecturing in Glasgow he had little thought that a young American would one day read his work and become so impressed with it, that he would have that first vision of divine love and the possibility of man's spiritual nature, that would become the master light of all his seeing.[26] This was William Ellery Channing, whose famous Baltimore sermon, delivered on the 5th May 1819, became the most widely read and influential sermon ever preached in America. In it he attacked the doctrine of the Fall, Original Sin, Predestination, Penal Atonement, and the Trinity. The Trinity, he said, was not in the Bible, leads to tritheism (three Gods), creates difficulties in worship, and distracts the mind in its communion with God. The two-nature doctrine of the Person of Christ makes him into two minds, two souls, and two wills; and vicarious Atonement elevates Jesus above God as the one who delivers men from the divine punishment.

Positively, Channing advocated Arianism, believing in the pre-existence of Christ and his miracles. Christ is a being distinct from God, inferior to God, and unable to do anything without him. He came to restore men from sin and bring them into a state of happiness by instruction in God's nature and works, promises of pardon to the repentant, and assistance to the pious. His death and resurrection signify his divine mission and guarantee a future life.

Channing stressed God's moral perfections: God cannot do anything contrary to his justice, goodness and holiness. He rejects the thought that he can ever be influenced by anger or seek for vengeance; God will only punish his children, however sinful, for their ultimate advantage.

While Channing believed in miracles, he nowhere stressed them as evidence of Christ's divinity.[27] He teaches that Christ's divinity was a revelation of the divine in man and that the appeal of Christianity is to the religious nature of man. Channing appears to be the first of the Unitarians who, while stressing the Bible, yet appeals to an inner light and an inner experience which was independent of the Bible. God's love, man's natural goodness, Christ's gospel, do not depend on the Virgin Birth or the Resurrection or on Paul's Epistles. These truths need no defence; they are true because the best in us knows them to be true. This teaching on miracles not being necessary to attest revelation was to lead others who followed Channing to deny them.[28]

Channing held that the main difference between the Unitarians and the Trinitarians in his day was how far reason was to be used in explaining revelation. According to Channing reason must determine whether religion agrees with itself, with man's moral nature, with his experience, with the order of the Universe, and with the manifest attributes of God. The idea that reason is darkened by the Fall, is to be set aside, for both natural theology and Christianity itself would fall to the ground if this were so. Reason is capable of judging revelation.

It was James Martineau (1805–1900) who carried through Channing's work in England. He started his ministry in Dublin in 1829, and his ordination speech in Eustace Street Church shows that he was still under the influence of eighteenth-century thought. His Arianism is there plainly set forth.[29] Martineau did not remain long in that position. The Bible and the Creeds were set aside and conscience and reason were established in their place. Thus he denied the deity of Christ because it was unreasonable and rejected the penal theory of the Atonement on moral grounds. He challenged the older Unitarianism as being illogical. It tried to interpret the Bible rationally, and believed that when it was so interpreted, it would be entirely in harmony with right reason and morality. But it was discovered that to accept reason and conscience must be to reject the Bible as being unreasonable and immoral. Hence Martineau insisted that Unitarianism must accept either the Bible or reason and conscience as ultimate authorities. He chose the latter.[30] Revelation as certified by miracles is now practically abandoned; and Martineau's famous book *The Seat of Authority in Religion* (London, 1890), places the foundations of religion in reason and conscience and the heart of man.[31]

In his understanding of the Person of Christ, he worked from an understanding of man himself. He held that there is a 'divine spark' in all men, and the closeness of man and God varies from one man to another. In the saints and prophets there is a close affinity to God, and in Jesus there is a perfect affinity. From this, Martineau was able to advance to the position that the Incarnation is true, not of Christ exclusively, but of man universally and God everlastingly. There is a living union between God and man and the difference between Jesus and other men is not one of kind but of degree. It is wrong to set Christ on a pedestal as the unique form in which God has entered humanity. All men have the earthly and heavenly form, and justice can only be done to Christ when it is said of all men what the creed says of him exclusively.

More advanced opinions than Martineau's however, were spreading in Britain at this time. They were coming in from the continent of Europe through the writings of David Friedrich Strauss (1808–74), Ernest Renan (1823–92), and from America by means of the writings of Theodore Parker (1800–60).

Strauss excelled in stripping away the supernatural from the gospel narrative and explaining everything in a natural way. In his *Leben Jesu* first published in 1835, he said that Jesus was a Galilean Jew, a disciple of John the Baptist, who continued John's work when he was cast into prison. Popular legend gathered about him in course of time 'wrapping the bandages of supernaturalism around the prophet of Nazareth'. The task of criticism must be to reject these legends and find the true person. He denied the Virgin Birth, Baptism, Transfiguration and Resurrection. Prophecy, miracle, Incarnation are set aside together with the uniqueness of Christ. Strauss interprets Christ, in the Hegelian way, as symbolizing mankind in its identity with God. It is a mistake to see the unity of the divine and the human in the life of an historical person. A better way is to regard the whole race of mankind as the realization of such a union rather than one man at a particular point of time.

But how are we to account for these fictional narratives in the Gospels? Strauss says that they are not there by dishonest trickery or gullible stupidity, 'but by an unconscious mythologizing process in which the supernatural and historical events recorded in the Gospels were all deduced from the Old Testament'.[32] They are the work of sincere men who thought it perfectly legitimate to demonstrate the fulfilment of the messianic prophecies of the Old Testament in Jesus.

His Hegelianism meant the replacement of a personal God by an impersonal Idea, 'the corollary of which was an Enlightenment cosmology in which the world was regarded as a closed system of natural laws allowing of no supernatural intervention from an other-worldly source'.[33]

Horton Harris points out how enormous was the influence of the *Life of Jesus*. It set in motion the whole 'Quest' for the historical Jesus which centered upon the problem of who Jesus actually was and it precipitated the great critical examination of the biblical sources. Above all Strauss was instrumental in influencing the course of the Old Testament studies for the Life of Jesus opened up a new interest in the Jewish background to the New Testament.[34]

74

But as Harris indicates, all Strauss' historical judgments were determined in advance by the philosophical presupposition that miracles do not and cannot occur, which in turn was derived from the prior presupposition that there is no transcendent personal God.[35]

Renan's work, being that of a novelist, was more popular than that of Strauss, but was even more fanciful. His book *Vie de Jésus* (1863), was highly imaginative, insinuating that Christ was forced by his disciples to play the role of a miracle worker and pretender to Messiahship. The disciples embellished the record of his life with legend. At first, Jesus was a simple teacher of natural religion preaching the Fatherhood of God and Brotherhood of Man. He intended setting up a Kingdom of God composed of Galilean sympathizers; but later in his teaching the Kingdom became more inward and spiritual.

In order to attract people Christ entertained greater ideas of himself and went as far as claiming divine honours. He adopted the role of a revolutionist and reformer and impressed the multitude with so-called miracles which showed his power over the minds of men. Since Easterners have a less delicate sense of fraud than we have, the disciples were quite ready to help Jesus out with these deceptions. This is seen in Martha, Mary, and Lazarus arranging to play a funeral for him at Bethany so that he might claim to be a resurrectionist. In due course, the disciples, carried away by their enthusiasm for him, actually raised the cry that he had been raised from the dead. Renan refers to the resurrection as the creation of Mary's love-sick heart that dreamed her Master back to life again.

It was Theodore Parker who popularised Strauss' ideas and widely influenced the Unitarians in the United Kingdom. In his books Parker argues for the immanence of God in man, rejects miracles, and considers Christ to be a mere man.[36] He speaks of Jesus, Mohammed and Moses in the one breath and holds that men as the brothers of Jesus have advanced further than he.[37]

He denied the Virgin Birth on the grounds of lack of historical evidence and the atoning sacrifice on moral grounds. It is true that Christ in his morality and example has set before man a pre-eminent likeness to God whose image he bore; but he was not sinless and was a child of his age in believing in a personal devil and demonical possession. Parker like Strauss and Renan excelled in pointing out deficiences and contradictions in scripture.[38]

In Ireland, particularly the North, a sustained attack was mounted on the doctrine of the Incarnation based on an exegesis of scripture. In the first half of the nineteenth century the debate centered around the interpretation of scripture and led to an Arian viewpoint; but in the second half of the century influenced by the thinkers mentioned above, the view changed to thinking of Christ as one of the greatest men who ever lived.[39]

They were willing to say that He possessed ample power, wisdom and understanding to carry out His mission; but that He did not possess them by His own inherent right. He was continually dependent for power, knowledge, guidance; and His message, mission, and authority were not His own but God's. His inferiority was shown by His worship of God. This view of Christ led to the denial of the doctrine of the Trinity.[40]

In general they opposed the two nature doctrine of Christ, the penal theory of the atonement, the depravity of man, the doctrine of predestination, the corruptions of Neo-Platonism which influenced the Apologists of the Church and led them away from basic scriptural teaching, the terminology of Chalcedon and that used in connection with Trinitarian doctrine, and justification by faith.

Finally, we notice parallels and differences between the movements which we have observed in this appendix and the position of the writers of the *Myth of God Incarnate*.

a) There is a denial of the Chalcedon Christology in both and there is agreement in rejecting the terminology involved.

b) Various groups of Unitarians particularly at the beginning of the nineteenth century would have accepted descriptions of Jesus such as we find in the mythographers, 'the supreme disclosure of God' or 'the embodiment of all God's promises brought to fruition'. In a day when they were not so troubled about Christianity's relationship to other religions, this was the way they described him.

c) They would agree that Chalcedon Christology created a cult of Christ and detracted from God. In fact the movement we have observed moved through all the persons of the Trinity and ended with Martineau's emphasis on the Spirit.

d) They would concur that the life of Jesus displayed an openness to God and that this would explain the relation of the two natures in a way Chalcedon could not. The high Arians of the previous centuries would agree that being in the presence of Jesus was like being in the presence of God. He was God's special servant and agent on earth.

76

e) As the movement we have observed developed the status of Christ changed and Arianism gave way to Unitarianism which laid emphasis on Jesus as a moral ideal which corresponds to what the mythographers at times say about him.

But in various ways the mythographers also differ, apart from their treatment of scripture, which reflects the use of Form and Redaction criticism and is not based on the propositional use of the Bible as in the Unitarian debates. They have not moved to the denial of the Trinity, though the traditionalists argue that this is the consequence of their work.[41] They seek to give Christ a high status and have not 'advanced' to the position of Theodore Parker. It will be a case of history repeating itself if they do in their future writing. Moreover, they are arguing about the problems of religious language and posing questions concerning the vexed question of the relation of Christianity to history.

In general the mythographers main problems centre on the use of myth as a valid terminology for expressing the truth of Christianity; how an act of God can take place in the light of modern historiography; and how we can put forward a Christology which will be acceptable in our pluralistic world.

It is these questions that have occupied our attention throughout this book.

77

APPENDIX 2

Christology

The mythographers argue that the traditional doctrine of the Incarnation meant, as we have seen, that a pre-existent mythological being (Logos or Son) joined himself with the man Jesus. They want to substitute the impersonal concept of the promise of God becoming embodied in the man Jesus as a more rational way of explaining how the divine and the human are related to his life and work.

They contend that the traditional doctrine of the two natures of Christ gives no satisfactory explanation as to how the Logos was united with the man Jesus without leading to a diminishing of the humanity.

This is a crucial question which they have raised and we want to show by a short historical background how difficult the Church found it to provide an answer to how the eternal Son and the Man Jesus were united. Having done that we will then proceed to consider more modern attempts to find a solution and try to clarify in a little more detail the solution which we outlined in Chapter Four.

First of all, however, we make brief mention of the Church's thinking on the relation of the Son to the Father.

The Christian Fathers followed the Greek concept of God and spoke of Him as unchangeable, impassible, and immoveable; but they developed the Logos terminology (Jo. i. 1) and wrote of the outgoing Logos or Word as well as the inherent Logos. This went a long way towards solving the problem of 'particularity' since everyman possessed potentially the Logos or reason within him. This universal, cosmic Logos which was acceptable to the Stoic philosophy became incarnate in the person of Jesus Christ.

However, it was the terminology of 'Father' and 'Son' which came to the centre of the stage since such terms were prominent in the biblical writings. This led to discussion as to how the relationship could be expressed. Origen argued that the Son was eternally begotten but was criticised because of his emphasis on the Son's subordination to the Father.

Theodotus contended for the man Jesus receiving divine power at his baptism (adoptionism) but not being different in kind from other men.

The Sabellians argued that the Father played three roles, Father, Son and Spirit, but were condemned because they had failed to distinguish the persons of the Trinity.

Arius in the Fourth century, as we have mentioned, said that the Son was like the Father but not of the same essence or nature; but Athanasius in opposing him contended that there could be no salvation without divinity. Finally the Cappadocians thought of the Godhead as one ousia with three hypostases. They worked in the context of Platonic ideas where the universal is more real than the particular, hence the stress was on the unity of God rather than the individual persons; the act of the one is the act of the other and any differences must lie in their inner relations rather than their action in the world. In contrast the Western tradition represented by Augustine emphasised the individual persons rather than the unity.

The mythographers have reminded us that such ideas of God based on Greek philosophy do not communicate with our world. However, it should not be forgotten that the concept of Incarnation received little support from such philosophy being absent from the writings and convictions of Platonism: how indeed could the eternal world of the forms come into contact with this imperfect and changing world? As Paul noted: "..... To the Greek foolishness ....." (1 Cor. 1: 23)

But there was always the thought of making Christianity more congenial to the philosophical temperament and this expressed itself in docetism: the Son of God only 'appeared' to take flesh (if he had it would have contaminated him) and in any case the divine left the human before crucifixion. The concept of adoptism had the same horror of the divine experiencing death and argued in the same way that such power left the earthly Jesus at this point.

These solutions to the problem were rejected by main stream Christianity; but before the thinkers of the Church lay the difficulty of demonstrating how divine and human nature could exist in the one person.[1]

Generally speaking, there have been two ways of describing the nature of Christ. One way follows the school of Alexandria and teaches that Christ is God living and acting humanly; the other follows the school of Antioch and holds that Christ is a Man in whom God lives and acts, or a Man fully indwelt by the Word of God.

The danger of the first is Apollinarianism,[2] the peril of the second is Nestorianism.[3] Some modern scholars have begun where Apollinarius began and stressed the reality of Christ's divinity. This is very true of Emil Brunner. Christ is the Eternal Word who comes to us from the other side. He is unique, coming to us from beyond the frontier of creaturely existence, and is essentially different from us.[4]

D.M. Baillie believed that Brunner's Christology led straight to Apollinarianism,[5] and Norman Pittenger insists that Christ's humanity holds no place in Brunner's system.[6]

In an attempt to avoid such criticisms, theologians who stress the divinity of Christ in the union of the two natures, have put forward the doctrine of Leontius of Byzantium that the humanity finds its person in the Word but is itself without a personal centre. This enhypostasis does not mean that the humanity is impersonal (anhypostasis) but as not having independent personality without the Logos. H.M. Relton argues for this point of view. He contends that without God, human personality is incomplete, and that He alone can supply it with that which alone can help to its full realization. Hence the manhood of Christ is more personal than any other man's because of its complete union with God.[7] George Hendry, however, points out that the enhypostasia when described psychologically verges on Apollinarianism. Once the divine 'person' who has assumed human nature without assuming human personality, is taken as a centre of consciousness or subject of experience, the doctrine becomes irreconcilable with the full humanity of Christ, since a human nature is inconceivable without a human personal subject.[8] He writes:

> "If Christ is true and complete man, it must be possible to raise the question of his person in terms of psychology and ethics, however difficult it may be to find the answers; for it is of the essence of manhood that it is susceptible to ethical and psychological interpretation. The doctrine of the incarnation means, that without prejudice to the uniqueness of Christ, his human nature and human experience are

open to the same modes of observation as those of other men. The humanity of Christ must be humanly interpreted, as the means by which God chose to deal with us humanly at the human level."[9]

Other scholars who begin with Apollinarius in stressing the deity of Christ, have sought an answer regarding His incarnate life in the kenotic theories. These take as their scriptural basis Phil. 2:7. The central idea is that the Son of God laid aside the divine attributes of omnipotence, omniscience, and omnipresence in becoming man. This does not mean that He was any less divine. It is merely the self-limitation of the eternal Son which was involved in His change of condition or environment, i.e. "the exchange of a spiritual mode of life in heaven for flesh and blood, the mere necessary conditions of an incarnation at all." But during this incarnation Christ possesses a full and true divinity.[10]

Likewise, the Reformation saw in Christ's humiliation a veiling or obscuring of His glory, but not a removal of His divinity in nature or exercise.

It is true that Luther, and the Lutherans, because of their doctrine of ubiquity, held the unusual view that the kenosis referred to the incarnate Logos and not the eternal Logos, but they agreed with the Church's tradition that Christ did not divest Himself of deity.[11] Modern advocates of the kenotic theory stress not the giving up the divine attributes but their operation in a new mode of existence. P.T. Forsyth said that in Christ we see the growth into a recovery of that mode of being from which, by His great act He came. He held that 'the diminuendo of the kenosis went on parallel with the crescendo of a vaster Plerosis.' He died to live.[12]

Moreover, attributes may be transposed and function in new ways. Christ possessed all the qualities of Godhead in potency rather than in full actuality. He gradually became aware of His divinity.[13]

Various objections have been brought against kenoticism. William Temple said that if the Creative Word was so self-emptied as to have no being except in the Infant Jesus then we are asserting cosmic chaos, for it means that the world was let loose from His control.[14] But if creation was carried out not by the Son but through Him, as the agent or medium, then God the Creator would be in control during the incarnate life of the Son. Nor does Temple's objection take notice of the idea that the divine attributes were possessed in the form of 'concentrated potency'.[15]

D.M. Baillie, for his part, objected that such theories meant a temporary theophany in which He who was God changed Himself temporarily into a Man. But, as we have seen already, the advocates of kenoticism insist on the reality of Christ's divinity, and point out that any theory of the Incarnation must reckon with the self-limitation of deity. Vincent Taylor goes as far as to see little difference between William Temple and the kenotics. Temple believed that God the Son, who is the Word of God, without ceasing His creative and sustaining work, added this to it that He became flesh, and dwelt as in a tabernacle among us.[16] This, as Oliver Quick commented, meant that what was added was precisely that experience in which His divine consciousness was limited and His divine state surrendered.[17]

A more pertinent objection is that kenoticism runs counter to the changelessness of God. This will hinge, however, on what our conception of this attribute is. H.R. Mackintosh would answer this objection by saying that what is immutable in God is His holy love which makes His essence;[18] and O.C. Quick would insist that it is the consistency of such love which is the very cause and ground of self-limitation.[19]

Vincent Taylor, arguing for kenoticism, puts forward the view that the divine attributes were not abandoned or destroyed but became potent or latent. It is better to speak of divinity as latent rather than concealed (Calvin) because the latter implies duality or even duplicity. Christ is divine, the Eternal Word, but in the form and under the conditions of human existence. The attributes are there in Christ and could be used at appropriate times. It is not essential that an attribute should be constantly operative, or, where potential is it necessarily destroyed. What Christ renounced would be the conscious exercise of such attributes. Taylor believes that the kenotic solution is the only one to the Person of Christ. As he says:

> "If the Son comes into the world omniscient and omnipotent, His coming is a theophany; He is downgraded to the level of a man. In the one case the humanity is a semblance; in the other the divinity is lost; in neither case is there a veritable incarnation of the Son of God."[20]

Other modern scholars, however, in their attempt to define the Person of Christ have started not with His divinity, but have followed Nestorius in beginning with the humanity. The manhood, they hold is perfect, fulfilling the idea of manhood, the proper organ of divine. Norman Pittenger in his book *The Word Incarnate*, 1959, is typical of this position. He disagrees with the 'neo-orthodox' school who cut the links between Christ and human experience and appear to present Jesus as a unique projection from eternity into time. He holds that enhypostasia really means anhypostasia.[21]

In propounding his own theory he has no difficulty in building a bridge between the divine and the human. Instead of Christ being different from humanity He must be looked upon in terms of the 'emergent' process philosophy. Jesus Christ is continuous with humanity, yet a genuine emergent bringing a 'new being' into which men are taken to be enlarged and enriched through their self-committal to Him. The Word in Jesus is the same which has through the ages constantly informed and moulded the world. Hence the life of Christ is 'the unique focus for a universal presence and operation'.[22] In the conclusion of his book he describes Christ as the One in whom God actualized in a living human personality the potential God-man relationship which is the divinely intended truth about every man. 'In Him that which is thus a possibility - and thereby the ground of our human existence; that which in each of us is to some slight extent partially realized and effectual and thereby the secret of our growth in true manhood; that is made real and factual'.[23]

It may be helpful at this point to reflect on the doctrine of the two natures of Christ which had its classic expression at the Council of Chalcedon in 451. The following is an extract:

> "We confess one and the same Son, our Lord Jesus Christ, perfect in Godhead, perfect in Manhood, truly God and truly man, of a rational soul (anti-Apollinarian) and a body, of one substance with the Father with respect to the Godhead (anti-Arian), and of one substance with us in respect of the Manhood (anti-Eutychian), like us in everything except sin; begotten of the Father before the ages according to his Godhead (anti-Arian) but in these last days begotten of the Virgin Mary, the God-bearer (Theotokos) according to his Manhood (anti-Nestorian), for our sake and for the sake of our salvation; one and the same Christ, Son, Lord, only begotten, confessed in two natures unconfusedly, unchangeably (anti-Eutychian), indivisibly, inseparably (anti-Nestorian); the distinction of the natures being in no way destroyed through their union (anti-Eutychian), but rather the peculiar quality of each nature being preserved and concurring in one Person and one Substance, not being parted and divided into two persons (anti-Nestorian), but one and the same Son and only begotten Son, the Word, the Lord Jesus Christ."[24]

Much criticism is directed mainly against the document which carried decisive weight at Chalcedon - Pope Leo the Great's letter to Flavian, popularly called 'The Tome'.[25] The document sets forth the alternation of the two natures in such a way that it portrays almost a 'Dr Jekyll and Mr Hyde' account of the life of Jesus. The life is presented as two lives, not easily conceived as the life of one person, one of them divine with all the supernatural attributes and the other human 'succumbing to injuries'. It is difficult to accept the doctrine in the form in which it appears in Leo's Tome.

In addition, Chalcedon has been criticised for a number of reasons. It is mainly negative, denying more than it asserts. While it condemns Apollinarius, Nestorianism and Eutyches, it does not give reasons why; nor does it (apart from the Tome) say how the Godhead and the Manhood are united. The categories used 'substance', 'essence', 'nature', 'hypostasis', sound strange to modern ears; and, as Paul Tillich says, we do not mean by human nature what they meant.[26]

The formula seems too static. It appears more interested in substance and metaphysic than subjects and persons. P.T. Forsyth said:

"..... We have come to a time in the growth of Christian moral culture when personal relations and personal movements count for more than the relations of the most rare and ethereal substances."[27]

In defence of the Chalcedon statement[28] it can be said that it is a principle rather than a theory. It leaves room for further theorizing, as long as we do not lose the truth that God and man are brought together in the Person of Jesus Christ. In other words, Chalcedon is a standard by which every theory must be judged.[29]

With that in mind it may be helpful to take note of the work of D.M. Baillie and that of Karl Barth. Baillie thinks that we should be guided by the Christian experience of grace in understanding Christ. Grace is seen when a man claims no credit for himself for any good that he has done, but ascribes all to God. Jesus is the greatest example of this:

"In the New Testament we see the man in whom God was incarnate surpassing all other men in refusing to claim anything for Himself independently and ascribing all to the goodness of God."[30]

Baillie differs from Pittenger in not seeing an ontological relationship between God and man, and in making the paradox of grace complete and absolute in Jesus so that the Life of Jesus is the very life of God Himself.[31]

Barth is against the Chalcedon formula because of its too static nature. He holds that any definition of the nature of Christ must take into account the entire fact of Christ.[32]

The Incarnation refers not only to the birth of our Lord but His whole life, death and resurrection. In short, the Person and the Work must not be divorced. Barth in his existential treatment of the doctrine of Christ brings the person into integral relationship with the work. He combines the doctrine of the two 'natures' with the doctrine of the two states of humiliation and exaltation, each of which must be interpreted in the light of the other. Humiliation and exaltation are not to be regarded as the successive stages in the history of Jesus Christ but as two sides of the work of reconciliation which filled His whole existence; they represent the actuality of the being of Jesus Christ as true God and true man. The Divinity of Christ is not to be defined in terms of an abstract and a priori conception of divine 'nature' but in terms of the dynamic concept of humiliation; and His humanity likewise in terms of exaltation.[33]

The merit of this treatment is that emphasis is laid upon both natures equally: not God without man or man without God, but Jesus Christ, the God-man.

Pannenberg shares with Barth this concern of understanding the two natures of Christ from the life, death and resurrection of Jesus and not from any speculations concerning an eternal Son.

We have tried to relate his thinking to the current controversy in Chapter Four. Here we need to reflect upon it again in a little more detail. We noted, on the basis of Hegel's definition of person, that Jesus is seen as the one who overcomes isolation and separation from others and God and attains a complete obedience and dedication to the Father. It was this which revealed his divinity. Hence he is the 'Son of God' in his humanity.

This seems to go some way in answering the criticism of the mythographers and others who cannot accept the union of the human and divine because they see it as a mythical descent of an eternal Son in becoming man. Hence the criticism that the humanity has become 'impersonal' by this union. But with Pannenberg what we find is a dependence and relationship to the Father not to an eternal Son.

Of course these arguments rest on the relational view of a person. This receives support from modern psychology which insists that the child develops its personality in relation to others. Thus we are active experimenters and not passive receivers and we need others to be ourselves. Descartes' "I think, therefore I am", is replaced by, "I participate, therefore I am."

Intellect of course is a way of sharing a union with others for I can share the thoughts of someone whom I am intimate with. But a much deeper union is affected by will. This requires not only action to please the other but obedience. Thus, as we have seen, the will of Jesus was dedicated to the Father and led to a life of complete obedience. That is not to say that his will was absorbed into the will of God, but that his will mirrored the will of the Father. Thus 'substance' in the traditional idea of union is replaced by a loving will.

This obedience unto the death of the Cross means that he is the 'Son' by which we realise, through grace and trust in him, our sonship. (Gal. 4: 5f; Rom. 8: 15). This redeeming aspect of the work of Christ again stresses his uniqueness.

But how does the idea of pre-existence enter in here? This pre-existence of an eternal Son was raised, as we remember in the Arian controversy and it is a problem for the mythographers. M. Goulder argues that it was due to Samaritan influence that the church came to think of Jesus as pre-existent and divine. However, New Testament scholars do not seriously consider this to be an explanation. Martin Hengel, with whom I discussed this matter in Tübingen, says that the theory is largely speculative and H.P. Owen has gone as far as to call it 'bizarre'. Of more weight is the exposition of scripture on this theme by Frances Young.[34]

She thinks that Paul teaches the pre-existence of a divine being in the letter to the Colossians (against a background of divine Wisdom) and in 1 Cor. 8: 6.

Further, the renunciation of a former superior status is found in 11 Cor. 8: 9 and Philippians 2: 5ff (cf. Rom. 8: 3). She thinks that Paul does not identify the figure with God but rather regards him as 'archetypal man' and 'archetypal Son of God' in whom men become sons of God.[35]

Again, after an exhaustive examination of the cultural background, in which she sees parallels everywhere with the concept of pre-existent beings she concedes that analogies with the Christian Incarnation concept are inadequate, for pagan mythology could only envisage a docetic Incarnation and Jewish legend could only think of the coming of an angel in disguise.[36] It is true that the "association of historical or contemporary personages with the appearances of the gods was occasionally made, but hardly seems to have been taken seriously."[37]

In commenting on her position here it would seem necessary to stress that this is what Christianity actually did and therefore exposed the movement to the dangers of mythology. In fact it has often been noted that within Christiantity such mythology took concrete form in Gnosticism which the New Testament condemns. But it would seem that, since they actually believed in the pre-existence of Christ, they felt that the danger was worth the risk. Nevertheless, Young is surely right in contending that, "the distinctive characteristic of mainstream Christian belief is its inability to stray too far from the historical reality of Jesus of Nazareth, a man crucified under Pontius Pilate." It was the implications of such a belief that led to the use of 'pre-existence', as an expression of his significance, rather than the applying of such a concept drawn from the environment to Jesus. At least this might be inferred from her discussion based on admission of no exact parallels.

Young, as we have seen, thinks of Jesus as "the embodiment of all God's promises brought to fruition", or "God's meaning was embodied in Jesus Christ (rather as we might speak of the Queen embodying British sovereignty) so that men had access to it through him." This is in the context of a discussion of pre-existence where she says that the term may mean an abstraction rather than a personality or some ill-defined combination of the two.[38]

However, she is never quite satisfied with her own conclusions and again modifies the statement about, "God's meaning being embodied", as not corresponding to what the New Testament is saying. At one point, like the Arians of the eighteenth century, she is satisfied with accepting pre-existence but interpreting it as a supernatural agent or transcendent man or last Adam. She, like them, argues that there is no fully developed doctrine of pre-existence in the Pauline writings; but it has never been asserted, at least from the advent of Higher Criticism, that the Bible explicitly teaches certain doctrines but that they are there implicitly. They are deductions (whether valid or not) from the scripture. Even those who think, however, that pre-existent means 'in the purpose and intent of God from all eternity' concede that for Paul it was impossible to imagine Christ's pre-cosmic existence as anything other than personal.[39]

She favours the description of Jesus as the last Adam and says that this means fulfilment and eschatological finality: Jesus inaugurated the End of history. Here she is in the company of Pannenberg, but thinks, like Wiles that such an eschatological version that he and Moltmann render, linked as it is to the cultural conditions of the ancient world and of Jewish and Hellenistic concepts, cannot be revitalised.

However, she admits that the writer of the Fourth Gospel is pointing in the direction taken by the patristic writers and concedes that the writer thought of the Logos as personal.[40] The concept 'Son' too reflects an exclusive and unique relation, but she appears to think that he is other than God.[41]

Nevertheless, this is high Christology, for Jesus must be regarded as Final. She notes that her position does not reduce the 'offence' of 'particularity' in Christianity, and would not make dialogue with other religions any easier than the traditional doctrine. This shows a difference from John Hick who thinks that a reinterpretation of the Christian myth, such as appears in the *Myth* book, would make Christianity more palatable for the adherents of other religions.

Let us, however, at this point, summarize objections to the view that Christianity derived its idea of pre-existence from the surrounding environment.

a)   It is doubtful whether in the pre-Christian period there existed a complete redeemer myth that was merely transferred to Jesus.[42] The Hellenistic concept of a divine being active from time to time on earth may have offered no more than a point of contact that secured an understanding of the Christian message.

b)   Pre-existence means that Jesus belongs to the sphere of God which was established through the revelatory character of his resurrection.

c)   In order for an 'influence' (Hellenistic thought) to be understood the following is to be observed: "The history of ideas is not a chemistry of concepts that have been arbitrarily stirred together and are then neatly separated again by the modern historian. In order for an 'influence' of alien concepts to be absorbed, a situation must have previously emerged within which these concepts could be greeted as an aid for the expression of a problem already present." The 'living situation' of these ideas in the New Testament is the eschatological character of the Christ-event.[43]

d)   The relation of the historical Jesus to his Father leads, when properly understood to the concept of pre-existence; but the latter can be retained only in critical reference to this root.[44]

e)   Only if the concept of Incarnation cuts itself loose from the Old Testament and Jewish theology of history, does it become a mere myth, a myth of a divine being descending from heaven and ascending again.[45]

If these theological arguments are acceptable is there any philosophical objection to the idea of a disembodied person? Plato of course had his concept of the pre-existent soul and recently an attempt has been made to state the Incarnation in relation to this concept.[46] Further, the idea of re-incarnation is very strong in Indian philosophy.

John Hick candidly admits that a person need not necessarily be embodied and also that there may be persons who are not human beings. He writes: "So it is thus far possible that a non-human person, namely God the Son, became humanly embodied as Jesus of Nazareth."[47] He goes on, however, to reject the idea, not on mythological grounds, but that it would make the temptations of Jesus illusory.

However that may be, does this problem not arise because we keep thinking of an eternal Son and the man Jesus as two separate beings? When we separate the union of Jesus with the Father by concentrating on an eternal Son then we are not taking into account what we said about the relation of the temporal and the eternal in Chapter Four. Further, we are engaging in mythical thinking. As Pannenberg writes: "it (the mythical) separates the essence of reality as a special, prototypal essence from the appearance in order to reunite the two through a dramatic process especially conceived for the purpose."[48]

Hence, we can distinguish the eternal Son of God from the man Jesus but only as two aspects of Jesus Christ. When we are aware that the mythical element of two separate beings in Jesus was aided by the Hellenistic category of the Logos, then we can counter this by tying Incarnation to the Old Testament, apocalyptic expectation, and the earthly life of Jesus. Having done this, we note that the Father-Son relation, that we know in retrospect and which always belonged to God's essence, now has acquired corporeal form.[49]

Therefore, incarnational affirmations are not mythological but functional, that is they are expressions of the truth gained from the perspective of God's eschatological revelation in Jesus.[50]

Notes

Chapter One

1. See the present writer's essays in *Les Églises et Leurs Institutions au XVIème Siècle,* Université Paul Valéry, Montpelier 1978; *Challenge and Conflict,* W. & G. Baird Ltd., Belfast 1981; 'The revolt against creeds and confessions of Faith', *Scottish Journal of Theology* Vol. 29.
2. M. Wiles, *Myth of God Incarnate* 1977, SCM, London.
3. D. Bonhoeffer, 'The non-religious interpretation of Biblical concepts' in *Letters and Papers from Prison* rev. ed. SCM, 1967 pp. 152ff., 178ff., 195ff.
4. Frances Young, *Myth,* p. 16.
5. M. Wiles, ibid p. 148ff cf. *The Remaking of Christian Doctrine,* SCM, 1974, p. 161f.
6. J. Hick, *Incarnation and Myth: The Debate Continued,* ed. M. Goulder, SCM, 1979, p. 84.
7. M. Wiles, *Myth* p. 162.
8. M. Wiles, *Debate* p. 212.
9. Thus myth as reflecting the universal connects with this way of viewing history.
10. See Wiles' article in *Theology,* Jan. 1978 and *What is Theology?* OUP 1976, p. 102.
11. R. Bultmann, *Kerygma and Faith* p. 42 cf. *Die Geschichte der synoptischen Tradition,* 1968, p. 160ff, 308ff. See also the present writer's article in *Theology* 1972.
12. This in general represents the position of the writers of the *Myth.*
13. M. Wiles, 'Does Christology rest on a mistake?' Ch. 10 *Working Papers in Doctrine,* SCM 1976, p. 122ff.
14. Often used by F. Young in *Myth.*
15. Wiles likes this view of Schubert Ogden which reflects ideas drawn from process theology. See Ogden, *The Reality of God,* London 1967; *Christ without Myth* London 1962.

16. See A.O. Dyson, *Who is Jesus Christ?* London SCM 1969, p. 74f for his views on process theology and his comments on the work of Teilhard de Chardin.

Chapter Two

1. M. Wiles, *Myth* pp. 1–5.
2. Ibid p. 153.
3. R. Bultmann, *Jesus Christ and Mythology*, SCM 1960, Criticism of Bultmann is in *Kerygma and Myth*, ed. H.W. Bartsch (Eng. tr. R.H. Fuller)
4. M. Eliade, *Myths, Dreams and Mysteries*, Fontana. See also *Myth and Reality*, "Is it even possible", he asks, "to find one definition that will cover all the types and functions of myths in all traditional and archaic societies?" *Myth and Reality* pp. 5–6. Quoted by J. Knox, *Myth and Truth* p. 4 Carey Press, London 1966.
5. A football commentator recently described the repeated meeting of two teams in a cup semi-final as a saga meaning not only length of time but as reflecting determination to win, endurance, loyalty etc.
6. N. Pittenger, *The Word Incarnate*, Harper New York 1959, pp. 39f. Cf. W. Pannenberg, *Basic Questions in Theology*, Vol. 111 SCM p. 71ff. Since Christianity has this historical connection, Ian Barbour prefers model to myth. Christ is a central model in the Christian paradigm (a tradition transmitted through historical exemplars). See *Myth, Models and Paradigms*, Harper and Row, N.York 1974, p. 24f cf. 150f.
7. Peter Stern, *Realism*, London 1973, p. 40. He recognises that the ministry and death of Christ are the most realistic of stories, p. 47.
8. Hans Frei, *The Eclipse of Biblical Narrative*, 1974, p. 16.
9. We need to take this point up in detail in chapter four. It is based on the useful philosophical distinction between 'knowing how' and 'knowing that'.
10. See A. Marwick, *The Nature of History*, Open University Press.
11. D.F. Ford, *Karl Barth* ed. Sykes 'Barth interpretation of the Bible', p. 105. Ford quotes Brian Wicker's *The Story-shaped World, Fiction and Metaphysics: Some Variations on Theme* London 1975, p. 105.
12. James Barr, 'Some thought on narrative, myth and incarnation' p. 15. in *God Incarnate Story and Belief* London SPCK 1981.
13. Ibid p. 16.
14. J. Knox, *Myth and History* p. 58f.
15. Karl Barth defines saga as "an intuitive and poetic picture of a pre-historical reality of history which is enacted once for all within the confines of space and time." p. 81 Church Dogmatics 111, i. Saga therefore deals with unique and unrepeatable events. Here we agree with Barth, but disagree that they happen in a 'time' which cannot be scrutinised by secular historians. This *Heilsgeschichte* or sacred history is protected by Barth's idea that it runs parallel with our history (historie) but cannot be investigated. But it is this theological interpretation which raises the problems as we will see in the next chapter. Moreover, some definitions of myth would include Barth's saga.

16. See the present writer's article on the 'Image of God' (Imago Dei) in *The Expository Times* Vol. LXXVII, No. 8 1966. Note however problems with God 'willing' in P. Davies, *God and the New Physics* p. 134ff J.M. Dent London 1983.

17. See Chapter One of this book p. 3.

18. William P. Alston, *Philosophy of Language*, p. 102f Prentice Hall, London, 1964. See Max Black for his useful discussion of metaphors in *Model and Metaphors* p. 31ff, Cornell University Press, Ithaca and London 1962. Also Mary Hesse's review of E.R. MacCormac, *Metaphor and Myth in Science and Religion*, Durham N.C. 1976 in *Scottish Journal of Theology* SAP Edinburgh Vol. 31 1978, p. 180.

19. That Jesus Christ was the Son of God and one in essence with God the Father. It was based on Greek metaphysics.

20. Martin Hengel, *The Son of God*, SCM 1976 p. 93. The present writer had the opportunity of discussing current English Theology with Professor Hengel at Tübingen in November 1980. He did not feel that this debate had changed his opinion as expressed in the above work.

21. Dennis Nineham, *The Myth*, p. 186ff.

22. Ibid.

23. Rachel Trickett, *God Incarnate Story and Belief*, ed. A.E. Harvey, SPCK, 1981, p. 39.

24. A. Harvey, Ibid p. 6.

25. J. Macquarrie, Ibid p. 30.

26. Ibid.

Chapter Three

1. Arthur Marwick, *The Nature of History*, OUP. (1970) I am indebted to this book in particular in considering the craft of the historian.

2. Thucydides (ancient Greek historian), Bede (eighth century), Voltaire and Gibbon (eighteenth century).

3. R. Bultmann, *Jesus and the Word* Charles Scribner's and Sons, New York, 1958. Bultmann argues that Jesus appeared at a time of apocalyptic expectation which expected a Saviour figure: Christ, Son of Man, David, etc. The New Testament is also influenced by the background of Gnosticism: personal redeemer figure who descends from heaven. Further influence was the divine/human figure who died and rose again. The 'preached' Christ is not identical with the Jesus of History. When truly preached he presents the individual with a choice i.e. existential decision to commit life to him. He makes extensive use of the philosophy of Heidegger. See *Being and Time*, E.T. J. Macquarrie and E. Robinson, SCM 1962.

4. Ibid.

5. A. Harvey, 'Christology and the Evidence of the N.T.' in *God Incarnate, Story and Belief* p. 49 SPCK London 1981.

6. See the present writer's article on the debate between Barth and Bultmann concerning the resurrection in *Theology*, 1972.

7. Members of the original society. It is interesting to note here that John Hick accepts the findings of parapsychology. At least in the sense of telepathy, and the idea of God acting in healing and in response to prayer. Such matters, he

thinks, lie beyond the vision of the physical sciences. See *Religion in S. Africa* Vol. 2. No. 1. Jan. 1981, p. 4.

8. E. Troeltsch was influential in pointing out the relativities of historical study. Such unique events as asserted by Christianity immediately came under suspicion. Troeltsch argued that the historian proceeds by analogy: the interpreting of the unknown of the past by the known of the present. Further he contended for the idea of correlation: "all historical happening is knit together in a permanent correlation.... Any one event is related to others." Therefore the historical and the relative are identical. See the *Absoluteness of Christianity* E.T. SCM London 1972 Translation of *Die Absolutheit des Christentums und the Religionsgeschichte* J.C.B. Mohr Tübingen 1929.

9. W. Pannenberg, *Jesus, God and Man*, SCM London 1980. pp. 90–95.

10. C. Moule in debate with Don Cuppit in *Theology*, p. 514.

11. A. Armitage, *The World of Copernicus*, p. 40. EP Publishing Ltd. 1972. He shows how Heraclides and Aristarchus thought of the earth moving round the sun.

12. T. Torrance, *Divine and Contingent Order*, OUP 1981.

13. E. & Marie-Louise Keller, *Miracles in Dispute*, SCM 1969.

14. M. Hesse, 'Miracles and the Laws of Nature' in *Miracles* ed. by C.F.D. Moule, Mowbray & Co. Ltd. London 1965. p. 38.

15. Hesse ibid. p. 39.

16. N. Smart, *Philosophers and Religious Truth*, SCM 1969. pp. 25ff.

17. Ibid.

18. W. Heisenberg, *Physics and Beyond* (1971) p. 237ff. Quoted by T. Torrance op. cit. p. 45.

19. J. Habgood, *Religion and Science*, Mills & Boon, 1965.

20. C. Vesey, *René Descartes, The Father of Modern Philosophy*, A100 Units 25 and 26, OUP Bletchley 1971.

21. Teilhard de Chardin, *The Phenomenon of Man*, Harper & Row, pp. 71ff.

22. John Greer, *Evolution and God*, CEM London 1979 p. 58. This is panentheism, a term used by John Robinson, Charles Birch, and W.H. Thorpe.

23. J. Macquarrie, 'Creation and Environment', *The Expository Times*. Vol. LXXXIII No. 1. pp. 6–8. Quoted by Greer, op. cit. p. 71.

24. O.R. Jones, 'Philosophical Reflections on Creation'. *Science and Religion* ed. by I. Barbour, pp. 229ff, SCM 1968 – I have used the analogy suggested by Jones but at times put it to different use.

25. Ibid – for a detailed critique of its defects see O.R. Jones' article.

26. I. Barbour, *Issues in Science and Religion*, SCM 1966 chapter 11.

27. L.C. Birch 'Creation and the Creator' p. 214 ed. I. Barbour op. cit.

28. C. Moule op. cit. p. 16.

29. C. Moule op. cit. p. 17.

30. Cf. Teilhard's Omega point.

31. A.D. Galloway, 'Wolfhard Pannenberg', in *The Expository Times* p. 70. Dec. 1980 Vol. 92. No. 3. The difference between Whitehead's view of God and Pannenberg's is brought out by the sentence from Pannenberg: "What turns out to be true in the future will then be evident as having been true all along". i.e. opposes Whitehead's view that the futurity of God's kingdom implies a development in God.

32. W. Pannenberg, *Jesus, God and Man*, p. 100.

33. M. Wiles points out that Pannenberg can only justify his claim that Jesus Christ has absolute significance in an eschatological context, that is that such significance could not occur in a relative process of history but only at the end of history. *Explorations in Theology* 4 SCM 1979, p. 20f.
34. T. Torrance op. cit. p. 24.
35. J. Macquarrie, 'Truth in Christology' in *God Incarnate Story and Belief,* p. 33 "....almost all contemporary theories of man, from Marxism at one end of the spectrum to Thomism at the other, have been stressing the 'openness' of human nature and its apparent indefinite possibilities of transcendence."
36. · A.D. Galloway, op. cit. p. 71.
37. Ibid.
38. Ibid.
39. D.S. Russell, *Apocalyptic Ancient and Modern,* SCM 1978, p. 20.
40. A.R. Peacocke, *Creation and the World of Science,* OUP, 1978, p. 329.
41. Ibid. p. 239.
42. G. Kaufmann, *God the Problem,* p. 241.
43. *Religion in the Making,* New York 1926, p. 32.
44. M. Wiles, *Working Papers in Doctrine,* SCM 1976, p. 146.
45. A.D. Galloway, *Wolfhart Pannenberg,* p. 44. Allen & Unwin London, 1973.
46. W. Pannenberg, *Basic Questions in Theology,* SCM 1971 E.T. of *Grundfragen systematischer Theologie,* Vandenhoech und Ruprecht, Göttingen 1967, Vol. 1. pp. 48, 76, Vol. 2. p. 113f.
47. Galloway op. cit. p. 61.
48. Ibid. P. 58.
49. Ibid. p. 47.
50. G. Hunnings, *Journal of Theology for S. Africa,* Vol. 35 June 1981, p. 72.
51. Galloway op. cit. p. 48,
52. P. Carnley, 'The Poverty of Historical Scepticism' in *Christ, Faith and History,* p. 165ff. W. Pannenberg has an interesting comment on Lessing's maxim that accidental truths of history cannot provide a proof for eternal truths of reason: "Do not his truths arise only when one abstracts what has happened out of its referential context and considers it as an isolated individual? And is it not an illusion to find in reason a source of truths which are removed from and superior to all historical conditioning." BOT p. 58 footnote vol. 1.

Chapter Four

1. E. Schillebeeckx, *Jesus,* Collins, London, 1979 p. 68.
2. H.D. Lewis, *The Elusive Mind,* 1972.
3. Schillebeeckx op. cit. p. 71.
4. Schillebeeckx op. cit. p. 72.
5. D.E. Nineham, *St. Mark,* pp. 50—51 Penguin, Middlesex, 1963
6. Ibid.
7. Schillebeeckx, op. cit. pp. 78—79.
8. Schillebeeckx, op. cit. p. 77.
9. F. Kermode *The Genesis of Secrecy,* pp. 118—9 London 1979.

10. Schillebeeckx, op. cit. p. 87.
11. Schillebeeckx, op. cit. p. 87.
12. See in particular the writings of P.F. Strawson and S. Hampshire i.e. *Thought and Action* 1960 Viking Press New York, 1959, and *Individuals*, London, Methuen, 1969.
13. Church Dogmatics, Vol. 2, Pt. 1, p. 331.
14. D. Kelsey, *The Uses and Abuses of Scripture in recent Theology*, SCM London 1975, p. 39.
15. R.H. King, *The Meaning of God*, SCM 1974, p. 10.
16. Nineham, op. cit. p. 71.
17. Nineham, op. cit. pp. 96–98.
18. Nineham, op. cit. p. 87. Quoting Montefiore.
19. Nineham, op. cit. p. 85.
20. Nineham, op. cit. p. 86.
21. Nineham, op. cit. p. 46.
22. There were other conceptions of a more supernatural king but generally this one prevailed.
23. The power Christology is ruled out. See Schillebeeckx, op. cit. p. 417.
24. Mk. viii. 11ff. It seems reasonable to argue that this was at least one of the reasons for the 'secrecy' emphasised by Mark.
25. Mk. x. 28ff.
26. Mk. iii. 31ff. See Nineham, op. cit. p. 122.
27. Mk. xiv. 36f. Schillebeeckx notes that as a fact of history it can hardly be doubted that Jesus was subject to an inner conflict between his consciousness of his mission and the utter silence of God. At least in its hard core as an event the struggle in Gethsemane is not to be cogitated out of existence. See p. 317 op. cit.
28. Nineham, op. cit. p. 122.
29. Schillebeeckx, op. cit. 477f.
30. Ibid.
31. Ibid p. 479.
32. Ibid p. 480.
33. Ibid p. 476. Bultmann recognises the historical character of Jesus' prophetic self-understanding on basis of Lk. xii. 19, Mk. ii. 17; Mt. xv. 24.
34. Ibid p. 183.
35. N. Perrin, *Introduction to the New Testament*, London SCM passim
36. Is. xxxv. 5–6.
37. A.E. Harvey, *Jesus and the Constraints of History*, Duckworth, 1982, p. 97.
38. Mk. vi. 46, Mt. xiv. 23, etc.
39. Schillebeeckx, op. cit. 259, 551.
40. Ibid p. 264.
41. See Schillebeeckx argument against Bultmann, op. cit. p. 301.
42. Mk. x. 45, Lk. xxii. 27. Cf. Jo. xiii. 1–20.
43. Schillebeeck, op. cit. p. 308.
44. Ibid p. 312.
45. Harvey, op. cit.
46. Mk. i. 1; Mk. ix. 7; Mk. xv. 39: Mt.xvi. 16.
47. J. Dunn, *Christology in the Making*, p. 243 SCM 1980 London.
48. Dunn, op. cit. p. 258–259.

49. Dunn, op. cit. p. 263.
50. Dunn, op. cit. pp. 264–265.
51. Pannenberg, *Jesus, God and Man*, p. 62 SCM London.
52. Pannenberg, *Theology and the Kingdom of God*, Philadelphia 1971, p. 51f.
53. Ibid p. 56.
54. Ibid p. 62.
55. A. Galloway, *The Expository Times*, Vol. 92. No. 3 Dec. 1980 pp. 69f.
56. A. Galloway, Wolfhart Pannenberg, Allen & Unwin, London 1973, p. 82.
57. Pannenberg, *Jesus, God and Man*, SCM London p. 141. 1980.
58. Ibid p. 153.
59. See present writer's article in The Expository Times, Vol. LXXIX, No. 1, 1967.
60. A. Galloway, *The Expository Times*, p. 72. Vol. 92, No. 3 Dec. 1980.
61. Present writer's article op. cit. See C. Stead on *Divine Substance* p. 267. H.P. Owen sees the disadvantages of using 'substance', *Religious Studies* Vol. 13 No. 4 Dec. 1977. D.M. Mackinnon sees 'homoousios' as a second order rather than a first order christological proposition, *Christ, Faith and History*, p. 279.
62. Apology, Ch. 21.
63. J. Hick, *Christianity at the Centre*, SCM London 1968. Now republished with significant change of title: *The Centre of Christianity*, 1977 to reflect change of views.
64. J. Hick, ibid, p. 37. Hick, however, has departed from this meaningful insight and now sees the love of God not as the essence of God but as one of his attributes. Other attributes could be manifest in other religions.
65. See the present writer's article in *Scottish Journal of Theology*, Sept 1967, Vol. 20. No. 3 for a discussion of the Trinity. Hegel is important here. For him the absolute is not substance but subject which exists only by emptying itself into what is other than itself. It is part of the nature of the absolute Spirit to reveal and manifest itself; that is, to be represented in the other and for others and itself to become objective. Pannenberg of course, uses Hegel in this regard and W. Kasper in his, *Jesus the Christ*, p. 183, sees the advantage of this. See Hegel, *Lectures on the Philosophy of Religion*, Humanities Press, Inc. 1962 vol. iii. pp. 24f.
66. Hick, ibid, p. 38.
67. Mk. i. 11, ix. 7; Mt, iii. 17, Mt, xvii. 5; Lk. iii. 32.
68. Pannenberg, op. cit. pp. 182–3.
69. K. Rahner, 'Jesus Christ' *Sacramentum Mundi, Burns and Oates*, London 1969 Vol. 3. p. 20. Quoted by D. Watson, *Journal of Theology for S. Africa*, p. 13 June 1982. Watson thinks that Chalcedon thought of a person in relational terms, but H.E.W. Turner insists that ancient thought concentrated on 'self-subsistence not on relations' *Jesus the Christ* p. 61f. 1978.

Chapter Five

1. O.C. Thomas, *Attitudes Towards Other Religions*, SCM, London 1969.
2. John Hick (ed.) *Truth and Dialogue*, Sheldon, London, 1975 p. 155.

3. H.P. Owen, *Religious Studies,* Vol. 13 p. 505. No. 4 Dec. 1977.
4. F. Young, *The Myth of God Incarnate;* John Hick, *The Myth*, p. 172, p. 119 cf. *The Debate,* 174ff.
5. K. Cragg, *The Christian and Other Religions,* Mowbray, London 1977 p. 76.
6. Reported by Dr. Almed Shafaat of the Nur al-Islam Foundation, Leicester, *Journal of Beliefs and Values,* Vol, 2, No. 2. 1981.
7. John Hick, *God and the Universe of Faiths,* MacMillan, London 1973 p. 176.
8. M. Wiles, 'Religious Authority and Divine Action' *Religious Studies* March 1971 p. 3ff.
9. W.J. Abraham, *Divine Revelation and the Limits of Historical Criticism,* OUP, 1982, p. 83.
10. K. Barth & E. Brunner, See *Natural Theology,* Bles. 1946.
11. J. Hick, *God and the Universe of Faiths,* p. 131.
12. G. Lampe, *God as Spirit* Clarendon, Oxford.
13. See Appendix 1.
14. Hick, op. cit. p. 147.
15. Hick, op. cit. p. 147.
15. *Scottish Journal of Theology,* Vol. 29. p. 69.
16. Ibid p. 71.
17. N. Smart 'Truth and Religions' *Truth and Dialogue* Sheldon 1975 pp. 51ff.
18. Ibid p. 55
19. P. Tillich, *Ultimate Concern,* SCM London, 1965.
20. Ibid. Tillich prefers Logos, however, to Christ.
21. P. Berger, *A Rumour of Angels,* Pelican, London 1969 p. 96.
22. *Church Dogmatics,* IV, 3(1) p. 124.
23. J. Moltmann, *Christianity and Other Religions* ed. Hick & Hebblethwaite pp. 202—203.
24. Ibid p. 109ff Paul Tillich's view.
25. Ibid p. 227 J.V. Taylor
26. David Martin disputes pluralism: "We live, some sociologists suggest, in a pluralistic society in which all views are relativised by competition. Curiously enough, I would argue that our religion is less pluralistic than it was in Victorian times. Enclaves of Hindus and Muslims and enclaves of middle class humanists do not in themselves necessarily make Britian a religiously pluralistic society. In fact, the religion of modern Britian is a deistic, moralistic religion-in-general, which combines a fairly high practice of personal prayer with a considerable degree of superstition." 'The Secularisation Question' *Theology* LXXVI No. 630 Feb. 1973. p. 86. Quoted by Gill *Social Context of Theology* Mowbrays London p. 122, 1975.
27. J. Hick in *Religion in S. Africa,* No. 12, Jan. 1981, p. 7.
28. Jo. 9. 32; Lk. 1. 34.
29. Jo. 20. 24.
30. R.G. Collingwood, *The Idea of History,* OUP, 1961, p. 9.
31. G. Hunnings, 'A Response to Martin Prozesky' *Journal of Theology for S. Africa,* Vol. 35, June 1981, 9. 72.
32. Abraham, op. cit. p. 124.
33. P. Berger, 'The Secularisation of Theology' *Journal for the Scientific Study of Religion,* p. 8. Cf. *The Heretical Imperative,* Collins London 1980.

34. Abraham op. cit. p. 129. See also evidence that A.E. Harvey produces for scepticism among ancient historians regarding miracles p. 102, *Jesus and the Constraints of History,* Duckworth, 1982 London.
35. T. Ling, *A History of Religion East and West,* Macmillan 1968 London p. 214.
36. *Myth,* p. 118.
37. R. Gill, op. cit. p. 129.

Appendix 1

1. Attributed to W. Chillingworth (1602–44). See his *Religion of Protestants,* Vol. 11 (London: H.G. Boan, 1846) p. 410.
2. *English History in Contemporary Poetry,* IV (London: G. Bell and Sons, 1913) pp. 40ff.
3. This was discovered in 1823 and published in 1825. Milton's anti-trinitarianism was unknown until the publishing of this work. See J. Milton: *Prose Works* (London, 1853).
4. Alexander Gordon speaks of him as the 'Socinus of his age'. A. Gordon: *Heads of English Unitarian History* (London, 1805) p. 2.
5. See *Essay concerning the Human Understanding* (London: W. Baynes & Son, 1823).
6. J. Habgood: *Religion and Science* (London: Mills & Boon, 1964).
7. L.C. Birch: *Nature and God* (London: S.C.M., 1965) p. 15.
8. Ibid. p. 15.
9. Ibid. p. 24.
10. I.G. Barbour: *Issues in Science and Religion* (London: S.C.M., 1966) p. 70. The present mythographers have been accused of Deism since they deny the idea of Incarnation.
11. L.C. Birth, op. cit. p. 16. Concerning Locke, Birch writes (p. 21): 'Probably no philosophical writings gave more reinforcement to deism than Locke's two works *An Essay concerning Human Understanding,* (1690) and *The Reasonableness of Christianity* (1695).
12. *The Reasonableness of Christianity as Delivered in the Scriptures,* London, 1810 pp. 224f. Cf. Chapter xi on the doctrine of scripture.
13. Alexander Gordon: *The Disciple,* Vol. III (Belfast, 1882) p. 365. J.H. Colligan in his book *The Arian Movement in England* (Manchester, 1913) says that Locke's influence in the matter of method was paramount.
14. *Essay Concerning the Human Understanding,* 1823, ed. Bk. IV, pp. 10.
15. A. Gordon: *Historic Memorials of First Presbyterian Church,* (Belfast, 1887) p. 32.
16. *The Scripture Doctrine of the Trinity,* 3rd ed. (London, 1732) pp. 234-235.
17. Ibid. p. 274.
18. *An authentic account of several things done and agreed upon by the Dissenting Ministers lately assembled at Salters' Hall (1719).* It should be noted, however, that the issue was subscription rather than the denial of the Trinity. Published in the *Christian Moderator* magazine (London, 1826–8) 2 vols., Vol. I, pp. 193–6.

19. *Heads of English Unitarian History* (London, 1895), p. 37; John Taylor: *The Scripture Doctrine of Original Sin,* 3rd ed. (Belfast, 1746); J. Taylor: *Atonement* (Belfast, 1751).

20. *Sermons on the Christian Doctrine* (Belfast, 1819). Edited by William Bruce. Published by the Presbytery of Antrim.

21. J.H.S. Burleigh: *A Church History of Scotland* (London, OUP, 1960), p. 288.

22. H.F. Henderson: *The Religious Controversies of Scotland* (Edinburgh, 1905) p. 11.

23. Burleigh, op. cit., p. 290.

24. Burleigh, op. cit., p. 295.

25. Op. cit., p. 296. The friendship of Leechman and Hutcheson lasted. It was Leechman who edited Hutcheson's lectures which were published by his son under the title: *A System of Moral Philosophy,* 2 vols. (Glasgow and London, 1755). See James McCosh: *The Scottish Philosophy* (London, 1875).

26. Anne Holt: *William Ellery Channing* (London: O.U.P., 1942) p. 9.

27. 'Divinity' is used here in the Arian sense.

28. R.E.B. MacLellan: *Discourse on the Death of William Ellery Channing* (Belfast, 1842) pp. 12ff.

29. *Address* at Ordination Service (Dublin, 1829) p. 27.

30. James Martineau: *Endeavours after the Christian Life* (London: British & Foreign Unitarian Association, 1907), passim.

31. J.E. Carpenter: *James Martineau* (London, 1905) p. 587: cf. Martineau's *Study of Religion* (Oxford: Clarendon Press, 1888); *Types of Ethical Theory* (Oxford Clarendon, 1885) 2 vols.

32. Horton Harris: *David Friedrich Strauss and his Theology* (London, 1973) p. 45.

33. Ibid. p. 277.

34. Ibid. p. 281.

35. Ibid. p. 283. If we hold the existence of a personal God, then as Harris says, we must seek to provide a better and more convincing explanation than Strauss (Ibid. p. 284).

36. *Theism, Atheism, and the Popular Theology,* Centenary edition (Boston); *Discourse of Matters Pertaining To Religion,* 3rd ed. (Boston, 1847).

37. *Discourse* p. 241.

38. Ibid. p. 245ff.

39. W.H. Drummond: *Theological Works 1829;* J.A. Crozier: *The Life of Henry Montgomery 1875;* H. Montgomery: *The Creed of an Arian;* J.S. Porter: *Unitarianism 1841.* See the present writer's Ph.D thesis on the Non-subscribers, Queens University, Belfast.

40. See the present writer's article in the *Scottish Journal of Theology,* Sept. 1967.

41. See Michael Green, *The Truth of God Incarnate* Hodder & Stoughton 1977. Stephen Neill asserts that the authors of 'Myth' are offering the old Unitarianism. See his essay 'Jesus and Myth' in the same work.

Appendix 2

1. Origen (185–253), Theodotus (second century), Sabellius (early third century), Arius was a presbyter of Alexandria, died 336, Athanasius (295–373), Basil (the Great) of Caesarea (330–379), Bishop of Caesarea in Cappadocia from

370. He with Gregory of Nazianzus and Gregory of Nyssa were known as the Cappadocian Fathers. See two books by H. von Campenhausen on *The Fathers of the Greek Church* and *The Fathers of the Latin Church* respectively published by A & C Black, 1963/4. G.L. Prestige: *Fathers and Heretics* (SPCK, 1948). J.N.D. Kelly: *Early Christian Doctrines* (A & C Black, 1958). W.H.C. Frend: *The Early Church* (1965, Hodder & Stoughton). The Library of Christian Classics (SCM, 1953) vol. 1–8. Maurice Wiles: *The Christian Fathers* (Hodder & Stoughton, 1966).

2. Apollinarius, Bishop of Laodicea in the fourth century, taught that the mind in Christ was taken by the divine Logos. This denied that Christ was truly man, for our minds are the distinctly human element in our nature. Apollinarius could not meet the objection that if the Logos was to redeem our human nature by entering into it, he must have entered into it at the very point where sin begins, i.e. the mind. The heresy was condemned by the Council of Constantinople in 381. Eutychus, a monk of Constantinople in the fifth century, also eliminated the humanity by teaching that the divinity swallowed it up.

3. Nestorius was Bishop of Constantinople in A.D. 428; it was said that he so stressed the humanity that it appeared separate from the divinity. There was no real union but only a kind of mechanical conjunction between the two. Hence Christ could suffer as a man, and yet as God be incapable of suffering. It missed the truth that God and man have been united in one Person; moreover, it made the mode of union no different from one of degree between Jesus and the prophets in whom also the Spirit of God had dwelt. Nestorius may have been misinterpreted. See *Book of Heracleides* (Eng. Tr. by G.R. Driver and Leonard Hodgson, 1915); cf. J.N.D. Kelly: *Early Christian Doctrines*, p. 317; H. Bettenson: *Documents of the Christian Church*, and R.V. Sellers: *Council of Chalcedon*, p. 237, n. 5.

4. *The Mediator*, Eng. Tr., 1934, p. 240.

5. *God was in Christ*, 1961, p. 90., Faber Edition.

6. *The Word Incarnate*. 1959, p. 142.

7. *A Study in Christology*, 1917. See present writer's fuller exposition of this view in 'Evangelical Quarterly' Vol. L111 – No. 4, 1981.

8. *The Gospel of the Incarnation*, 1959, p. 88. In *Essays in Christology for Karl Barth*, Chalcedon is interpreted through the enhypostasia.

9. Ibid, p. 91., cf. D.M. Baillie, op. cit., pp. 90–93.

10. J. Ernest Davey: *The Jesus of St John*, p. 163.

11. Thomasius was the first advocate of kenoticism. He held an emptying of certain divine attributes only and that for a period. Gess thought Jesus lost His eternal self-consciousness and only gradually regained it in the course of His ministry. Ebrard taught that the Logos reduced Himself to the dimensions of the human soul without ceasing to be the eternal Son. Modern advocates are A.B. Bruce: *The Humiliation of Christ*, 1876; A.M. Fairbairn: *Place of Christ in Modern Theology*, 1893; Bishop Gore: *Dissertation on Subjects connected with the Incarnation*, 1898; P.T. Forsyth: *The Person and Place of Christ*, 1909; H.R. Mackintosh: *The Doctrine of the Person of Jesus Christ*, 1912, etc.

12. *Person and Place of Jesus Christ*, 1911.

13. Vincent Taylor: *The Person of Christ in New Testament Teaching*, 1958, p. 477.

14. *Christus Veritas,* 1924.
15. Taylor: op. cit., p. 267.
16. Op cit., p. 140.
17. *Doctrines of the Creed,* p. 138.
18. Op. cit., p. 470.
19. Op. cit., p. 135.
20. *The Person of Christ,* p. 294.
21. Op. cit., p. 101.
22. Op. cit., p. 192.
23. Others who appear to follow Pittenger in starting from the humanity of Christ are those who call Him 'the symbol of God' (C. Hartshorne: *Reality as Social Process,* 1953), or 'The Personality of God' (C.J. Webb: *God and Personality*), or 'The Inspiration of God' (W.R. Matthews: *The Problem of Christ in the 20th Century,* 1950).
24. *Nicene and Post-Nicene Fathers,* Vol. XII, pp. 38–43 (Letter XXVIII).
25. But see O.C. Quick: *Doctrines of the Creed,* for defence of the Tome, (Fontana) Ed. 1963, p. 133.
26. *Systematic Theology,* Vol. II, p. 167.
27. *The Person and Place of Jesus Christ,* 1911, p. 331ff. Both he and H.R. Mackintosh favour the idea of a progressive incarnation. See Mackintosh: *The Doctrine of the Person of Christ,* p. 496ff., cf. Leonard Hodgson: *Christian Faith and Practice,* 1950, p. 68.
28. It has been ably defended by J.L.M. Haire in *Essays in Christology for Karl Barth,* 1951, edited by Parker 'On Behalf of Chalcedon'.
29. Alan Richardson: *Creeds in the Making,* 1935, p. 85. cf. John Burnaby: *The Belief of Christendom,* 1960, p. 82.
30. Op. cit., p. 117.
31. See Pittenger's criticism, op. cit., p. 197.
32. This has affinities with the *Heilgeschichte* theology of Oscar Cullmann. In his *Christology of the New Testament,* Eng. Tr. 1959, Cullmann analyses the titles given to Christ in the New Testament and shows that the Christology of the early Church was founded upon the words and deeds of Jesus. The experience of the early Church, the presence of the Holy Spirit, and their own reflection, led them to see cosmic implication in the historical work of the Master. It is seen as God Himself in His revelation. The New Testament supplies us, not with abstract categories such as substance or nature concerning the being of God; its revelation is historical, therefore its Christology is *Heilgeschichte.* Hence Christ must be explained, not in terms derived from Greek philosophy but in Biblical terms such as 'event'. See pp. 3–6, 181, 235, 306f.
33. *Kirkliche Dogmatik* IV, 1, p. 146 (*Church Dogmatics,* pp. 133f).
34. M. Goulder, *Myth,* p. 64f.
35. *Myth,* p. 21.
36. *Myth,* p. 119.
37. *Myth,* p. 119. John Hick sees parallels between the incarnation of a pre-existing Son or Logos and the incarnation of the pre-existing heavenly Buddha. See *Religion in South Africa,* vol. 2, No. 1, January 1981, p. 7.
38. *The Debate* (ed) Goulder, p. 181. Here the reference is to the Logos.

39. G.B. Caird: 'The Development of the Doctrine of Christ in the New Testament' in *Christ for us Today* (ed) N. Pittenger (SCM, London, 1968) p. 80.
40. *Debate,* p. 179.
41. Ibid, p. 182.
42. Pannenberg, *God and Man,* p. 151. He is dependent upon C. Colpe's book, *Die religion geschichtliche Schule: Darstellung and Kritik ihres Bildes vom gnostischen Erlösermythus* (Göttingen, 1961).
43. Ibid, p. 155.
44. Pannenberg, ibid. Footnote p. 155.
45. Pannenberg, ibid. p. 157.
46. James Moulder: 'Journal of Theology for South Africa' No. 35, June 1981.
47. John Hick, ibid. p. 24.
48. Pannenberg op. cit. p. 154.
49. Pannenberg and Moltmann agree that 'the order of knowing' and 'the order of being' are to be distinguished. Thus the disciples knew after the resurrection what was true from the beginning.
50. Pannenberg, op. cit. p. 157.

Index

Abba 43f
Abraham W.J. 97, 98
Act of Uniformity 69
Acts of God 6, 57
Adoptionism 14
Agent 44
Alston W.P. 92
Anhypostasis 80
Anti-Trinitarianism 66
Apocalyptic 20, 30, 31
Apollinarianism 80
Arian 1, 66, 67, 70, 76, 86, 87, 99
Arius 79, 99
Armitage A. 93
Athanasius 79, 99
Atomic Particles 24
Augustine 74

Baillie D.M. 80, 81, 84, 100
Barbour I. 91, 93, 98
Barr J. 12, 91
Barth K. 39, 60f, 84, 85, 91, 92
Basil (the great) 99
Beethoven 27
Being of God 26
Berger, P. 63, 97
Birch L.C. 93, 98
Black M. 92

Boethius 53
Bonhoeffer D. 90
Bruce A.B. 100
Bruce W. 99
Brunner E. 80, 97
Buddhism 56, 58, 59, 61
Bultmann R. 5, 9, 16, 63, 90f, 91,
    92, 95
Burleigh J.H.S. 71, 99

Caird G.B. 102
Calvin J. 1, 68, 81
Carlyle A. 72
Carnley P. 94
Cappadocians 79, 99
Carpenter J.E. 99
Certainty 33f
Channing W.E. 72, 73
Chardin T. de 91, 93
Chillingworth W. 67, 98
Chopin F. 27
Christian Fathers 78 ff
Christians 19
Christology 7, 16, 42, 52, 53, 54, 77,
    80ff, 88, 95, 101
Clarke S. 70, 71
Colligan J.H. 98
Collingwood R.G. 97

Comte A. 20
Consummation 13
Council of Chalcedon 50
Cragg K. 56, 97
Creation 13, 28, 29
Creative Activity 27
Crozier J.A. 99
Council of Chalcedon 83
Council of Constantinople 100
Cullman O. 101

Darwin C. 27, 66
Davey J.E. 100
Davies P. 92
Deism 23, 27, 68
Descartes 26, 39, 85
Deterministic 24
Docetism 79
Drummond W.H. 99
Dunn J. 46, 95, 96
Dyson A.O. 91

Einstein 33
Eliade M. 91
Enhypostasis 80
Environment 4, 64f
Eschatology 29f, 31, 42, 64
Euclid 33
Eutychus 100
Evolution 13
Evolutionary view of the world 4
Experiments 25

Fairbairn A.M. 100
Ford D.F. 12, 91
Form Criticism 11, 36, 38
Forrester D.B. 58
Forsyth P.T. 82, 84, 101
Fourth Gospel 2, 16, 46, 59, 60
Frei H. 91
Freud 57

Galileo 68
Galloway A. 33, 34, 49, 93, 94, 96
Gess 100
Gethsemane 45
Gill R. 97, 98
Gnosticism 46, 48, 86, 92
Gordon A.S. 70, 98

Goulder M. 86, 101
Green M. 99
Greer J. 93
Gregory of Nyssa 51

Haire J.L.M. 101
Hampshire S. 95
Habgood J. 93, 98
Harris H. 74, 75, 99
Hartshorne C. 101
Harvey A.E. 42, 92, 95, 98
Hegel 47, 53, 85, 96
Hegelianism 74
Heisenberg W. 25, 93
Henderson H.F. 99
Hendry G. 80
Hengel M. 86, 92
Hesse M. 92, 93
Hick J. 55f, 58, 65, 89, 90, 92, 96,
    97, 102
Higher criticism 87
Hinduism 57, 58, 59, 61
Historical approach 18ff, 34, 36
Hodgson L. 101
Holt A. 99
Hume D. 25
Hunnings G. 94, 97
Hutcheson F. 71f, 99

Identification 11, 38f, 42f
Immanence of God 27
Incarnation 2, 4, 5, 24, 46, 52, 55, 62,
    64, 66, 75, 78, 81, 85, 86, 88, 89
Intention/action 35, 39ff, 40
Isaiah 27, 42
Islam 55, 56, 58, 59, 61
Israel 5, 14, 29, 31, 32, 33, 41, 44, 55

James W. 21
Jesus Christ, passim
Jones O.R. 93

Kant I. 31
Kasper W. 96
Kaufmann G. 94
Keller E & M 93
Kelsey D. 95
Kenoticism 81, 82
Kermode F. 94

104

King R.H. 95
Kingdom of God 30, 42, 45, 49
Kinsey Report 33
Knox J. 91
Krishna 58, 59

Lampe G. 97
Laws of nature 24
Leechman W. 71, 72, 99
Legend 9
Leo 83
Leontius 80
Leprosy 40f
Lessing 94
Levels, higher and lower 25, 28
Lewis H.D. 94
Light waves 52
Ling T. 98
Literal 14
Locke J. 67, 68ff, 98
Logos 27, 46, 50, 59f, 78, 79, 80,
    82, 87, 89, 100, 101
Love of God 15, 52
Luther M. 1, 82
Lutherans 82

MacCormac E.R. 92
MacLellan R.E.B. 99
Mackinnon D.M. 96
Mackintosh H.R. 81, 101
MacQuarrie J. 16, 92, 94
Mark J. 41, 42, 45
Martin D. 97
Martineau James 73, 74, 76, 99
Marwick A. 91f, 92
Matthews W.R. 101
McCosh J. 99
Messiah 41, 69
Metaphor 3, 14
Milton J. 67, 68, 98
Miracles 4, 24f, 72f, 75
Miracle stories 42
Mohammed 55, 59, 61, 64, 75
Moltmann J. 87, 97, 102
Montgomery H. 99
Moulder James 102
Moule C. 93
Myth 2, 8ff, 14, 32, 88, 90

Nature 24
Neill S. 99
Nestorianism 80, 84
Nestorius 82, 100
Newton I. 23f, 68
Newtonian 25, 33, 68
Nineham D.E. 37, 92, 94, 95
Non-Subscribers 1, 66 ff

Observer 24
Ogden S. 90
Openness to world and God 30
Origen 79, 99
Owen H.P. 86, 96f, 97

Pannenberg W. 46f, 49, 85, 87, 89, 91,
    93, 94, 96, 102f
Parable 3
Parker T. 74f, 77, 101
Particular 32
Paul 21f, 22, 23, 45, 46, 52, 59,
    60, 63
Peacocke A.R. 94
Perrin N. 95
Pittenger N. 80, 82, 84, 91, 101
Plato 89
Platonic ideas 79
Platonism 79
Porter J.S. 99
Price R. 71
Pre-existence 78, 86ff
Pre-scientific 4, 20
Process philosophy 83
Psalmist 27
Psychosomatic 21

Quick O.C. 81, 101

Rahner K. 96
Realistic narrative 10, 13, 37
Reformation 1, 82
Reimannian 33
Relationships 38f
Religious Experience 57
Relton H.M. 80
Renan E. 74, 75
Revelation of John 31
Richardson A. 101
Robinson J. 93

Russell D.S. 94

Sabellians 79, 99
Saga 9, 10, 12, 13, 14, 16, 32, 91
Schillebeeckx 38, 42, 94,95
Schweitzer A. 30
Scientific world view 62
Scotus Duns 53
Shafaat A. 97
Sidgwick H. 21
Simson J. 71
Smart N. 59, 93, 97
Society for Psychical Research 21
Son of God 3, 14, 15, 42, 45, 48, 50,
    53, 56, 79f, 81, 85
Stead C. 96
Stern P. 91
Strauss D.F. 14, 62, 74, 75, 99
Strawson P. 95
St Victor Richard 53
Substance 51
Suffering 41, 44
Symbol 3, 60

Taylor J.V. 97, 99
Taylor S. 70f
Taylor V. 81f, 101
Temple W. 81, 82
Tertullian 51
Theodotus 79, 99
Thirty Nine Articles 69

Thomas O.C. 96
Thomasius 100
Thorpe W.H. 93
Tillich P. 84, 97
Time 48
Torrance T. 93f, 94
Transcendence of God 27
Trickett R. 92
Trinity 1, 2, 52, 71, 72, 76, 77,
    79, 98
Troeltsch 93 ·
Truth 16, 30, 49
Turner H.E.W. 96

Unitarianism 1, 58, 66f, 69, 73, 77, 99
Universal 32

Vesey C. 93
Violation 24

Watson D. 96
Webb C.J. 101
Weiss J. 30
Whitehead A.N. 32
Wicker B. 12, 91
Wiles M. 87, 90, 91, 94, 97, 100
Will of God 41, 44, 45
Wisdom Christology 46f
Wittgenstein 63

Young F. 55, 64, 86, 90, 97